Emperor of Rome Marcus Aurelius, Meric Casaubon

The golden Book of Marcus Aurelius

Emperor of Rome Marcus Aurelius, Meric Casaubon

The golden Book of Marcus Aurelius

ISBN/EAN: 9783743322271

Manufactured in Europe, USA, Canada, Australia, Japa

Cover: Foto ©ninafisch / pixelio.de

Manufactured and distributed by brebook publishing software (www.brebook.com)

Emperor of Rome Marcus Aurelius, Meric Casaubon

The golden Book of Marcus Aurelius

THE LIBRARY
OF
THE UNIVERSITY
OF CALIFORNIA

GIFT OF

PROFESSOR

LEON J. RICHARDSON

THE
TEMPLE
CLASSICS

Edited by
ISRAEL
GOLLANCZ
M.A.

Marcus Aurelius
from a Bust in
Museo Nazionale Naples

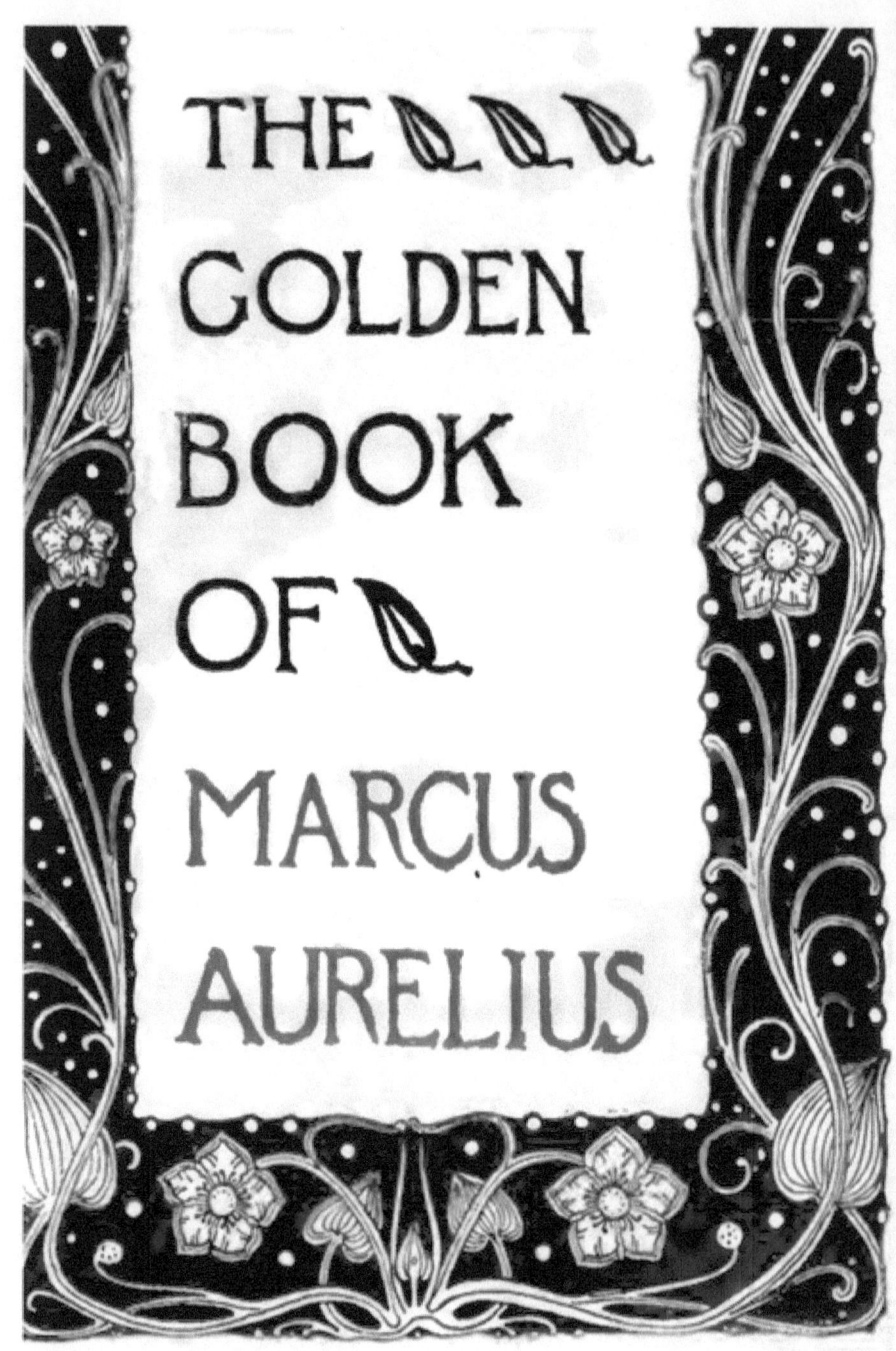

THE GOLDEN BOOK OF MARCUS AURELIUS

MDCCCXCVIII · PUBLISHED · BY · J · M · DENT · AND · CO: ALDINE · HOUSE · LONDON · E · C ·

MARCVS AVRELIVS ANTONINUS

THE ROMAN EMPEROVR,

HIS MEDITATIONS
concerning HIMSELFE:

TREATING OF A NATVRALL Mans happinesse; Wherein it consisteth, and of the meanes to attaine unto it.

TRANSLATED OVT OF THE Originall Greeke; with Notes:

BY

MERIC CASAVBON, B. of D. and Prebendarie of CHRIST Church, Canterbury.

The second Edition; with a TABLE containing the principall matters in the Booke.

ECCLVS. 18. 8.

What is man, and whereto serveth he?
What is his good, and what is his euill?

LONDON,
Printed by M. FLESHER, for RICHARD MYNNE, in Little Britaine at the Signe of S. Paul.

M DC XXXV.

To the most R. Father in God,
WILLIAM
BY THE DIVINE PROVIDENCE,
Lord Archbishop of Canterbury,
Primat of all England and Metropolitan;
One of the Lords of his Majesty's Most Honorable privie Councell;
and Chancellor of the University of Oxford:
My very Honourable good Lord.

May it please your Grace,

I Præsent here unto you the Writings of a King. I have presumed that you would honour that sacred Name even in a Heathen so farre, as to accept of the worke, were it but for the Authors sake. For as it may well be esteemed (in such an age as this) none of your Graces least commendations, that you are truly φιλοβασιλεὺς; so I suppose your selfe account it no small happines, that you live to serve so Great and Gratious a King. But if the bare Name of a King would not serve, I could add, that they are the writings of the Wisest, the Learnedst, the Best that ever was among Heathen Kings, if Historians may be credited. It is observed by some of them as a great argument of the Divine Providence, that such a

Wisdom, Learning, Integrity
Prince was provided against such times, when all things seemed to tend to ruine and confusion, and all human ordinarie meanes were thought too little to keepe the Empire standing: the happy preservation whereof they generally ad-scribe to the singular and extraordinarie Wisdome of this One; both in his Warres, abroad; and in his Civill government, at home. Hence it is, that as of a man of whome there is no hope, wee commonly say, *Ne Salus quidem:* so was it used as a Proverbe in after-ages by some of them, of a State irrecoverably gone, and declined, *Ne Marcus quidem.* As for his Learning, I could wish your Grace had the leasure to peruse the historians owne words, least myne may seeme too hyperbolicall, and yet come far short of their expressions. What shall I say then of his Integritie, which is so commended by them, as it alone might well be thought sufficient without any other commendation, to make him Incomparable? And indeede I feare I have spoken but improperly, when I have mentioned his Wisedome, Learning, and Integrity, as three severall Excellencies, since that (as he Himselfe professed, and they report of him) all the Learning he was ambitious of, was but to be Wise; and all the wisedome, but to be good. The writings of such a one, I know your Grace would respect, although he had beene no King. And yet another reason, which hath made me the bolder to present them to your Grace is, because in reading them you shall often reade your selfe; and though perchance your Modestie

will not suffer you to make the application, yet others will, I am sure, that shall reade him, and I could not but have respect unto it. Upon these reasons I have presumed. If beyond reason, I have no other excuse of my boldnes, but as I am,

A modern instance

Your Graces

humbly devoted Chaplain,

Meric Casaubon.

SOME FEW TESTIMONIES CONCERNING ANTONINUS, AND THESE HIS BOOKES.

Out of SUIDAS.

MARCUS the Romane Emperor; whom it **His Life** is easier to admire in silence then to praise, it being altogether impossible to equall his merits with any expression of words. For from his youth having betaken himselfe to a composed, and setled course of life, hee was never seene to alter his countenance, through either feare or pleasure. Hee most approved the Stoicks, not only in their order and discipline of life, but also in their course and method of learning. He therefore from his younger yeares, became so famous and illustrious, that Adrianus intended oftentimes to settle the Empire upon him: but having after a more legall way first setled it upon Antoninus Pius, hee neverthelesse reserved the succession of it unto Marcus. He thought good also by marriage to ally him unto Anton. Pius, that so by succession of blood also he might come to the Empire. As for Marcus, he still continued in the same private course of life, and in the like subjection as other Romans did, and was in nothing altered by this adoption, and new

Athena-　affinity. And when he was come to the Empire,
goras　and had the absolute power in his hands, he was
never knowne to doe any thing insolently, but as
in matters of bounty he was alwaies most free,
and exuberant; so in his government, he was no
lesse meeke and moderate.

Againe out of the same.

MARCUS Antoninus a Romane Emperour, having deserved in all things the commendation of a perfect Philosopher, &c. Hee hath written concerning the course of his owne life, twelve Bookes.

Athenagoras, a Philosopher of Athens, in his Apologie for the Christians addressed unto Marcus Antoninus, and his sonne Commodus, by way of humble Mediation and Intercession.

I Know well enough, that ye doe not more surpasse others in royall power and prudence, then in the exact perfection of all manner of learning: so that even they that have singled out, and wholly applied themselves to any one part, have not attained to that happy perfection in that one, which ye have attained unto in all parts of learning.

Iul. Capitol. in vita Marci.

ERAT enim ipse tantæ tranquillitatis, ut vultum nunquam mutaverit mærore vel gaudio, Philosophiæ deditus Stoicæ, quam et per optimos quosque magistros acceperat, et undique ipse collegerat.

TESTIMONIES and others

Vulcatius Gallicanus in Avidio Cassio.

NEC defuere qui illum [*Cassium,* scil.] Catilinam vocarent; cum et ipse gauderet se ita appellari, addens futurum se Sergium, si Dialogistam occidisset, Antoninum hoc nomine significans; qui tantum enituit in Philosophia, ut iturus ad bellum Marcommanicum, timentibus cunctis ne quid fatale proveniret, rogatus sit, non adulatione sed serio, ut præcepta Philosophiæ ederet, &c.

Aurelius Victor, in Breviario.

TANTUM Marco sapientiæ, innocentiæ, ac literarum fuit, ut is Marcommanos cum filio Commodo, quem Cæsarem suffecerat, petiturus, Philosophorum obtestantium [vi] circumfunderetur, ne se expeditioni aut pugnæ prius committeret, quàm sectarum ardua et occulta explanavisset. Ita incerta belli in ejus salute doctrinæ studiis metuebantur; tantumque illo imperante floruere artes bonæ, ut illam gloriam etiam temporum putem.

Is. C. Exercit. in Bar. pag. 85.

MULTA in hanc sententiam scribit M. Antoninus Imperator, in suis illis divinis libris, &c.

[Idem ad ista Iulij Capit: ridens res humanas, &c.] Non ridere, sed ritè, ac suo pretio æstimare res humanas solitus hic vir sapientissimus. Hoc ille nos docet, divinis illis suis libris: velut cum ait in 11. non enim tempero mihi, quin mellitissimi doctoris verba adscribam, &c.

Canterus Nou. Lect. lib. 7. cap. 1.

Canterus MARCUS Aurelius Antoninus, imperator optimus, atque idem philosophus tantus, ut hoc meruerit proprium cognomen, duodecim conscripsit *de officio suo* libros, maximæ pietatis, humanitatis, temperantiæ, eruditionis, aliarum rerum præclararum testes plenissimos; et cum quibus multorum philosophorum operosa præcepta collata, merito sordere possint. Quocirca nemo, spero, malè collocatum tempus putabit, quod in ejus operis lectionem studiosè quondam impendimus, cùm ex eâ præter cætera, fructum hunc retulerimus, quod ex multis vitiosis locis duo saltem dextro, si dicere licet, Æsculapio sanavimus. Ac primum sub finem primi lib. ait, τὸ μὲν ἐπὶ πλέον με προκόψαι ἐν ῥητορικῇ καὶ ποιητικῇ καὶ τοῖς ἄλλοις ἐπιτηδεύμασι, repetitur autem ἀπὸ κοινοῦ, παρὰ τῶν θεῶν ἔλαβον, sed pro μὲν, ego μὴ legendum affirmare non dubito. Nam ideo mox subjungit hæc, ἐν οἷς ἴσως ἂν κατεσχέθην, εἰ ᾐσθόμην ἐμαυτὸν εὐόδως προϊόντα. Quod si, inquit, in poeticis et oratoriis studiis fæliciter progressus fuissem; nemo me inde retrahere, et ad maiora perducere facile potuisset. Quocirca Diis gratias ago, quod in studiis illis non nimis magnum feci profectum, nec ea nimis adamare cœpi. Nec iniuria Imperator. Nam ut in homine privato tolerari fortassis queat, si natura iubente, suppetente otio, aspirante fortuna, iucunda Musarum studia paulo diutius colat, et amœnissimas sirenas, quæ tamen non dent sine mente sonum, attentius ac pertinacius auscultet; Ita non potest is, quem ad res maximas gerendas, ac totius Vniversi Canterus curam natura progenuit, alio cogitationes omnes suas, quàm ad eum scopum dirigere, et ut illum assequatur quàm citissime, non omnem operam dare. Sed iam ad alterum pergamus locum. In fin. lib. sexti, hanc adfert similitudinem, (vi. 50) εἰ κυβερνῶνται οἱ ναῦται ἢ ἰατρεύονται οἱ κάμνοντες κακῶς ἔλεγον, ἄλλῳ τίνι ἂν προσεῖχον, ἢ πῶς αὐτὸς ἐνεργοίη τὸ τοῖς ἐμπλέουσι σωτήριον, ἢ τὸ τοῖς θεραπευομένοις ὑγιεινόν; Quemadmodum, inquit, si nautæ gubernatori, aut ægroti medico maledicerent, non facilè alium auscultarent„ nec vel ille vectorum salutem, vel hic ægrotantium sanitatem procurare posset: ita cum quis alius nunquam alteri bene et recte monenti parere consilium capit, is **non** temere **vel** rectum vitæ cursum **tenere,** vel **post errore** in viam possit redire. Verum quod pene oblitus eram, pro κυβερνῶνται et ἰατρεύονται (Xylander), legendum est κυβερνῶντα καὶ ἰατρεύοντα. Quod cum non advertisset interpres, alioqui doctissimus, quique paucos hac ætate pares habet, alienum planè sensum commentus est. Sed profecto homines omnes sumus, et erramus facilime: nec reperitur hoc sæculo quisquam, qui securus possit medium Momo digitum ostendere.

[In the second edition Casaubon adds the passages where Suidas cites our author.]

TO THE READER

THIS Booke (of what worth I say not; but more men, I feare, will commend it, then will know how to make use of it:) after it had for so many ages undeservedly beene buryed in darknesse, is now first, **if** I may not say brought unto light, yet at least made common and intelligible. Twice it is true, within these 80. yeares it hath already beene set out in its owne originall Greeke: and set out both times with a Latin Translation, much revised and corrected in the latter edition. Yet such are those editions, both of **them**, so confused, **and** so corrupt; and such **is the** Translation in both the Editions, so imperfect often, and impertinent; that I say not so absurd and erroneous, as that it is not easie to determine, whether it be harder to understand Antoninus his meaning by the Greeke that is printed; or the Greek that is printed, by the Translation **of** it: but **that** of both we may boldly and peremptorily conclude; of the one, that it cannot possibly bee understood, as it is printed; and of the other, that it would be more for the credit of the Author (a man otherwise acknowledged very learned :) if wee did take no notice **of** it at all. I must adde besides, that there hath beene many yeares agoe a certaine Booke, first written in Spanish, and since translated into Italian, French, English, and **how** many tongues

The ear editions of this book

xv

The learned Spaniard more I know not; pretended by the Title to be a Translation of M. Aurel. Antoninus. But that the Author of it, (a learned Spaniard) was in good earnest, I could never have beleeved, and would have thought I had done him great wrong to say it, had not I read his Prefaces, where he so earnestly by reasons, such as he could finde, goes about to make his Title good, and as earnestly expostulates with men for their incredulity, who did not take his reasons for current and cleere ones. I cannot but commend his intention, which certainely was to doe good; but his way I much abhorre, and wonder as much at his judgement and discretion. Sure I am that by his whole booke it doth not appeare, that hee had ever so much as seene that himselfe, which his Title doth promise unto others, M. Aurel. Antoninus his booke: which either must bee this here, or none. For besides this, there is not any other, that ever was extant. For as for those other writings of his, which either he himselfe in his second booke, or Capitolinus in his life, or Nicephorus in his Ecclesiasticall Historie (lib. 3, cap. 31.) or any others mention, they mention them as books written, and composed by him, but not as ever publikly extant; which if they had, Suidas, or whosoever they be, whom Suidas in his Dictionary, in the word Marcus, doth alleage, would not have omitted them. Thus much I thought good here briefly to acquaint the Reader with; who if he please, may receive further satisfaction by the ensuing Discourse.

A DISCOURSE BY WAY OF PREFACE:

Concerning the Use and Subject of this Booke: The Author Antoninus; and this Translation of it.

Of all the severall sects and professions of Philosophers that ever were knowne or heard of in the world, there was not any that ever did hold maximes and opinions so contrary to flesh and blood; never any that was judged even by the learned Heathens themselves (witnesse learned Plutarch, who hath written a whole Booke of this very subject:) so grossely and manifestly to oppose nature, and to overthrow all grounds and principles of humane sense or reason, as the Stoicks did. And yet of all sects and professions, never any, that either with the best was of more credit, or with the vulgar more plausible. So plausible and popular, that there have beene times, when the number of the Stoicks alone, did exceed all the followers and professors of all other sects being put together. A thing the more to be wondred at, because that for that very reason, Christianity (though nothing so harsh in comparison:) hath ever by them of contrary professions, beene much opposed and contradicted.

The Stoicks

The 'End' of Stoicism

Of this a maine reason I conceive to have beene, that the Stoicks, though by their particular Tenets and opinions, they might seeme of all others most to oppose nature, yet that which they proposed unto themselves as the end of their lives, and the ground of all their Philosophie; that which they did ever sound in the eares of men and presse them with, was τὸ κατὰ φύσιν ζῆν, to live according to nature. Μέμνησο ὅτι ἡ φιλοσοφία μόνα θέλει, ἃ ἡ φύσις σου θέλει (v. 9): 'Remember that philosophie requireth no more at thy hands, then what thine owne nature doth require, and leads thee unto:' saith Antoninus. πῶς ὠμόν ἐστι μὴ ἐπιτρέπειν τοῖς ἀνθρώποις ὁρμᾶν ἐπὶ τὰ φαινόμενα αὐτοῖς οἰκεῖα καὶ συμφέροντα (vi. 27); 'What a cruell and unnaturall thing would it bee to restraine men from the pursuite of those things, which they conceive to themselves and their owne nature, most proper and convenient?' So they all speake, and that which they all generally did most beate upon, was this. Now whether the particular meanes which they did commend and propose unto that end, were indeed proper and naturall unto that end, unto which they did propose them, I will not here dispute. For the end, whether true or pretended, is that which men usually take most notice of. As for the meanes, how direct or indirect to that end, is not so easilie discerned. Their end therefore, being of it selfe so plausible and acceptable, I conceive it to have beene the thing especially, which made their doctrine and philosophie so too. And I am as verily persuaded, that a conceit and opinion many Christians have, that most of those things which are reproved in them as sinnes and vices, agree best with their natures; and many, if not most, of those duties that are required of them as Christians, are against, not depraved and corrupted only, which is not properly nature; but absolutely against the nature of man: and in generall that divine law and humane sense and reason, are things contrary and opposite; is that as much as any thing that doth discourage them from the intent, practice, and study of those things, which they by their profession cannot but acknowledge themselves bound unto. For it is not more naturall to a man to love his owne flesh, (which the Apostle witnesseth, 'no man ever hated:') then to love nature, and what he conceives to bee according to nature. Though it bee not so, yet if hee conceive it so, he affects it naturally, and in time it becomes naturall unto him indeed.

Virtue, Vice, a Nature

Now concerning Christianity, I know it is the opinion of many, that, matters of Faith and the Sacraments only excepted, there is nothing in the whole Gospell which is not *juris naturalis*, and most agreeable to humane reason. For my part, as I would not take upon mee, to maintaine their opinion precisely true in all points, and circumstances; so I must needs say, if wee esteeme that naturall, which naturall men of best account by the meere strength of humane reason, have taught and taken upon them to maintaine as just and reasonable, I know not

PREFACE

Christian precept not contrary to nature

any Evangelicall precept, or duty belonging to a Christians practice, (even the harshest, and those that seeme to ordinary men most contrary to flesh and blood, not excepted), but upon due search and examination, will prove of that nature. I say upon due search and examination. Many have touched upon this point, rather to shew the way unto others, then by way of undertaking themselves: among others, of late, the best able that I know now living to performe this or any thing else that belongs to a generall and compleat Scholler, Mr Hugo Grotius, in his collection and Translation of Greeke sentences. There be too, I know, that have undertaken much in this kinde: but of whom (as many as I have seene:) I may boldly say (and the more boldly because I name none:) that in many respects they have performed but little. I wish it with all my heart, that some able and judicious man would thinke it worth his labour and paines: were it but to this end, that the harshnesse which many Christians (though Christians, yet flesh and blood they will say) doe conceive to be in many divine precepts, might bee mollified and lessned, when it shall appeare that the very same things did not seeme harsh to them, that (in comparison of them whom God hath called by more speciall and supernaturall illumination:) were nothing but flesh and blood. That they who as men can so hardly prevaile upon themselves to strive against nature, and to yeeld to those things which they conceive against all humane sense and reason; might be **The Subject of this Book** of another minde, when they shall see that mere naturall men, who in humane sense and reason, of all others most excelled, have both esteemed themselves bound by nature, and others most unnaturall that refused, to follow or to forbeare those very things: *ut quivis arbitretur* (saith Minutius F., though upon another occasion) *aut nunc Christianos philosophos esse, aut philosophos fuisse jam tunc Christianos.* But not to prosecute this generall any further at this present: Of all Bookes in this kinde that ever have beene written by any Heathens, I know not any which either in regard of it selfe, (for the bulke thereof;) or in regard of the Author, deserves more respect, then this of Marcus Antoninus; **sonne** by **nature** of Annius Verus (a **man** of great qualitie in Rome) and adopted sonne of Antoninus Pius, a Romane Emperour, whom also hee succeeded in the Empire about the yeare of our Lord 162, or 163. The chiefest subject of the Booke, is, the vanity of the world and all worldly things, as wealth, honour, life, &c. and the end and scope of it, to teach a man how to submit himselfe wholly to God's providence, and to live content and thankfull in what estate or calling soever. But the Booke, I doubt not, will sufficiently commend itselfe, to them who shall bee able to read it with any judgement, and to compare it with all others of the same subject, written either by Christians or Heathens: so that it bee remembred that it was written by a Heathen: that is, one that had no other knowledge of any

The Author of the Book
God, then such as was grounded upon naturall reasons meerely; no certaine assurance of the Immortality of the soule; no other light whereby he might know what was good or bad, right or wrong, but the light of nature, and humane reason. Which though it were, (such as it was) from God the Author of nature (as what is not?) yet in regard it was not by any revelation, or any other extraordinary meanes, is therefore called humane and naturall. As for the Booke it selfe then, to let it speake for it selfe; In the Author of it two maine things I conceive very considerable, which because by the knowledge of them, the use and benefit of the Booke may bee much the greater then otherwise it would bee, I would not have any ignorant of. The things are these: first, that he was a very great man, one that had good experience of what he spake; and secondly, that he was a very good man, one that lived as he did write, and exactly (as farre as was possible to a naturall man,) performed what he exhorted others unto.

For the first, I have alwayes thought that it was not without Gods especiall Providence, that of all them that once were the peculiar people of God, hee was chosen to write against the vaine pleasures and delights of this world, who of all the rest had had most knowledge and experience of those things, that hee did write against. A poore man may from his heart perchance declaime against the vanity of wealth, and pleasures; and a private man, against the vanity of honour, and greatnesse; it may be from their hearts, but it is ever suspicious, and therefore of lesse power and efficacie. Suspicious I meane, that they are angry with that they would faine, and cannot get themselves; yea, and perchance inveigh of purpose, that by inveighing (an ordinary thing in the world :) they may get that which they inveigh against. But at the best, that they make a vertue of necessitie; that they speake against they know **not** what; and though they meane sincerely, as now; yet if they were in place themselves, God knowes what minde they would be of. And the event indeed, doth justifie these suspicions but too often. But when a man shall heare such a one as Salomon was, speaking in this manner : 'I said in my heart, Goe to now, I will proove thee with mirth &c. I made me great workes, &c. I made me gardens and orchards, &c. I made me pooles of water, &c. I got mee servants and maidens, &c. I gathered me silver and gold, &c. So I was great, &c. And whatsoever mine eyes desired, I kept not from them, I withheld not my heart from any joy, &c. Then I looked on all the workes that my hands had wrought, and on the labour that I had laboured to doe; and behold, all was vanitie and vexation of spirit, and there was no profit under the Sunne.' Is there any man so bewitched, and besotted with worldly wealth and pleasure, whom such a confession from such a one, will not move for a while at the least? And if this of Salomon, who at first had received such measure of Grace and illumination from God, that it may be more justly wondred,

<small>Solomon's confession</small>

Antoninus' confession that he ever did anything contrary to this profession, then that he should professe so much; how much more should that confession of Antoninus move us, dilated here by him and inlarged into xii. bookes, and briefly expressed and summed up in these words of his eight Booke. πεπείρασαι περὶ πόσα πλανηθεὶς, οὐδαμοῦ εὖρες τὸ εὖ ζῆν. οὐκ ἐν συλλογισμοῖς, οὐκ ἐν πλούτῳ, οὐκ ἐν δόξῃ, οὐκ ἐν ἀπολαύσει, οὐδαμοῦ (viii. 1). 'Thou hast already had sufficient experience, that of all the things that hitherto thou hast wandred and erred about, thou couldst not finde happinesse in any of them: not in syllogismes, and Logicall subtilties; not in wealth, not in honour and reputation; not in pleasure: in none of all these.' Of Antoninus I say, a meere Heathen, lead by humane reason only; Antoninus a man for worldly wealth and greatnesse so farre greater then Salomon, as Lord and Master I dare say of more great Kingdomes, then Salomon was of great townes in all his Kingdome; Antoninus, a man for his goodnesse and wisedome, by all men during his life, had in that honour and reputation, as never man either before him was, or (that we know of) ever after him.

But his goodnesse was the second consideration. It hath ever beene the complaint of all ages: There hath ever beene store enough of men that could speake well, and give good instructions: But great want of them that either could, or so much as endeavoured, to doe as they spake and taught others to doe. And what is the good that such can doe? The only good

PREFACE

What is virtue? I can conceive, is, that they perswade men as much as in them lies (and they goe very effectually about it:) that τὸ εὐσεβὲς τοῦτο καὶ ὅσιον παρὰ τοῖς πολλοῖς ἀνθρώποις λαλούμενον, κατάψευσμα ἐστιν ἀλαζόνων ἀνθρώπων καὶ σοφιστῶν, ἢ νὴ Δία, νομοθετῶν εἰς φόβον καὶ ἐπίσχεσιν τῶν ἀδικούντων. 'That all this that we call vertue and godlinesse, so much spoken of amongst men, are but words and emptie sounds; that there is no such thing really existent indeed, as piety and justice, but that it is a meere figment of some cunning juglers and impostors, or at the best a pretty device of Law-makers, and founders of common-wealths, to keepe silly people in awe and feare.' Can any man thinke otherwise (if otherwise he be not better grounded): that shall heare them speake and then looke upon their actions? Such therefore in my judgement might deserve farre more thankes if they did forbeare, and would rather lose the commendations of either a smooth tongue, or a ready pen, then to incurre both the just suspicion of being Atheists themselves, and the certaine guilt and crime of having made many others so. **Be it** therefore spoken to the immortall praise and commendation of this famous Antoninus, that as he did write so he did live. Never did writers so conspire to give all possible testimonie of goodnesse, uprightnesse, innocency, and whatsoever could among Heathens be most commendable, as they have done to commend this One. They commend him, not as the best Prince only, but absolutely as the best man, and

PREFACE

Ancient
repute
of the
Christians best Philosopher that ever was. And it is his proper commendation, that being so commended, hee is commended without exception. If any thing hath ever beene talked against him, the Historians mention it but as a talke: not credited by them nor by any that ever were of any credit. Thus the Heathens of Him. The Christians had but little reason to speake well of him, as having suffered many cruell persecutions under him: And in this case how free they have beene (some of them:) even with all extremity to enveigh against other Emperors, though much commended and magnified by the Heathens, is not unknowne. Yet I find not that ever they could fasten anything upon our Antoninus, whereby to staine his reputation; that ever they did so much as object unto Him, these many and grievous persecutions which they did suffer under him, as his owne act, or charge Him therefore of crueltie. And though it be granted, that Antoninus gave way to those persecutions, which certainly he could not altogether be ignorant of; yet to them that know the state of those dayes, it can be no wonder, that such a thing should happen in the dayes of such a Prince as Antoninus was. When Christians, besides the infamy of many horrible crimes, as common incest, homicide, &c. which (such was the power of calumny:) lay upon them; were generally accounted no better, then meere Atheists and Epicures. For indeed Atheists, Christians, and Epicures, were commonly joyned together as names, if not of the

PREFACE

same signification, yet of very great affinity, and hardly distinguished by the vulgar, but that of the three, the Christian was thought the worst. *Antoninus did as he wrote* Let it be then Antoninus his commendation, the greater and the more incredible in this age, the more the age is full of dissimulation and hypocrisie, that he was not (as now they rightly stile themselves, whom the common received Names of Christians, and Protestants will not content, such is their Zeale and puritie they thinke:) a Professor: as he spake and wrote, so he did. His meditations were his actions. His deeds (so still you remember Him a man and a Heathen) did agree with his sentences. Ὅτι οὐ προσποιητὸς ἀλλ' ἐξ ἀρετῆς πάντα ἔπραττε πρόδηλον, &c. And againe, ὡς ἀληθῶς ἀγαθὸς ἀνὴρ ἦν, καὶ οὐδὲν προσποιητὸν εἶχε, &c. 'That hee did not only as he spake, but what he did, he did it out of meere love to vertue. That it was a cleere case, which no man doubted of, that hee was in very deed a good man; so incapable was he of any dissimulation.' So Dio of him, and so others. And now that I have spoken so much of Antoninus his life, it will not bee amisse to say somewhat of that surname the Philosopher, which by many hath beene given and appropriated to this Emperor. In so much as Xylander, though he found it **not at** all (as he confesseth) in his MS. yet thought it fitting to adde it in the Title, and Inscription of these bookes as his proper and usuall Cognomen. But sure enough it is (as hath beene observed **by** learned men:) that this Title of Philosopher

What was a Philosopher? was never taken by Antoninus himselfe, nor given unto him by others, as a proper surname, as his father Antoninus was surnamed PIUS, and others otherwise, but only as a deserved Elogium and testimonie, at the discretion of them that either did speake unto Him, or wrote of Him. And so indeed it was very commonly, and even by those learned and Pious Christians, that directed Apologies unto Him for the Christians, adscribed unto him as an Elogium, and Testimonie; just indeed and deserved, but arbitrary and not proper unto Him, by way of a Cognomen or surname.

But, an Elogium and testimony of what think you? of his great learning (as we take learning now:) and progresse in the Sciences? Read him himselfe, and judge how much he would have esteemed such a commendation. A man would thinke, if Heathens, through their ignorance of the true God, and of his truth, had beene mistaken in the true application of words of praise or dispraise, that wee, by the helpe of a better light, might have rectified them, and not followed their examples. But now it is fallen out quite contrary. Who they be that the holy Scriptures usually call wise; who they to whom they adscribe knowledge and understanding; and who they are, who by them are termed fooles, blinde, ignorant, and the like, is not unknowne unto any. So spake the Ancient Heathens, when they would speake properly. He that was an honest upright, vertuous man, without dissimulation and hypocrisie, though he were such a one as had never beene brought up to learning, yea such a one as could neither read nor write, was their σπουδαῖος, πεπαιδευμένος, φιλόσοφος, their good scholler, their learned man, their Philosopher. His life and his actions, were all that they stood upon, though indeed they were of opinion, that it was very difficult, if not altogether impossible, for a man to come to the knowledge, of that which was right and wrong, just or unjust, and by consequent of true vertue, without much studie and paines taking. On the other side, an unjust man, a cunning, an intemperate; in generall, a vicious man, was their ἀπαίδευτος, ἀμαθής, ἰδιώτης, their Illiterate, their Ignorant, their Idiot. The most ordinary distinction was, of an Idiot, and a Philosopher. Neither was this the proper language of the Stoicks (which sect our Antoninus was much addicted unto:) but of the Platonicks likewise, and of most others. But the maine and principall property, whereby they did distinguish a Philosopher from all other men, was that he did all things μετὰ τῆς ἀναφορᾶς, with a relation unto God and his Providence ἀφορῶν εἰς τὸν θεόν ἐν παντὶ μικρῷ καὶ μεγάλῳ, as Epictetus (in Arrianus) speaketh. This you shall finde that Antoninus doth much stand upon. For indeed they did esteeme it the very character and essentiall note of a philosopher. In so much as that if any man seemed never so just and upright in his actions, yet if it were not μετὰ τῆς ἀναφορᾶς, they esteemed him little more than a meere Idiot.

Much more I had here to say concerning this *and the opposite?*

Of this Transla-tion

Of this matter, both in defence of Plato (whose **name** hath much suffered through some mens ignorance of the true sense of this word Philosophus) and for the clearing of many obscure places of Antoninus, which otherwise I thinke will hardly be understood. But because I feare it would make the bodie of this Preface to swell too much beyond the proportion of the rest, and that in the Notes it will come in well enough, I will reserve it unto that place.

Now for this my Translation of Antoninus, which is the last thing wee are to speake of, were it so that this Booke were as commonly knowne, and as easie to be got as many others of lesse worth are, I should bee well content to spare my labour, and referre it wholly to the judgement of the Reader. But for as much as by my owne experience I know the Booke, (though twice printed,) to be so rare, that it is not to bee found in many private studies, and sometimes not for many yeares together, in any Booke-sellers-shop: (I was beholding to learned Mr. Holsworths well furnished library for the first sight, and long use of the latter and better Edition; as also for the use of many other Bookes:) and that the Latine Translation of Xylander, hath beene commended and approved by the most learned (*doctissimus; eruditissimus Interpres; vir profundæ eruditionis*, &c. So they speake of him:) I doe think it very necessary, both that I should give the Reader that satisfaction that I doe not *actum agere*, and doe my selfe that right, that whereas I take upon me to translate Marcus Antoninus

Augustus, I may not be suspected to have translated Guilielmus Xylander Augustanus. Indeed and of Xylander's what might be expected from Xylanders Interpretation, may be collected by his owne ingenuous intimation, both in his Preface, where he is faine to Apologize for it, that he durst undertake it, professing that *in quibusdam* hee was constrained, to *divinare et audacter à codice Græco aut usu communi recedere;* as also in his Notes, where his words are *Sunt autem passim permulta, in quibus ariolo magis quam Interprete opus sit:* And that he doth so indeed, it doth but too manifestly appear by his Translation. For I dare boldly say, and doe him no wrong, that sometimes in a whole page, he hath not two lines of Antoninus his sense, and meaning. Besides the liberty that he takes unto himselfe to supply of his owne head, to leave out sometimes words, sometimes lines, to change and alter at his will; without any reason given for it, or so much as the Reader acquainted with it. And whereas Xylander puts the fault of all this upon the corruption and imperfection of the copie, I cannot any wayes approve it. For first, as I confesse the faults and corruptions of it, if in the printed copies they have not beene made more, then they were in the Manuscript (which I doe not beleeve :) to be many, so of those many, I know none or very few, that may be termed incurable. And as for the *Lacunæ* of it, I hope that they neither in this Translation (and what ancient booke is there almost but hath some?) will not be found many. As for any greater *hiatus*, as perchance of many

The leafes together, if any shall suspect the Copie to
Text have beene defective in that kinde, the method
and composition of the booke being such, that
it doth for the most part consist of certaine
Aphorismes and Canons, (they called them
κάνονας, θεωρήματα, δόγματα, κομματικούς
λόγους, &c.) without any certaine order or
series, either in regard of the whole (but that
they all tend to one purpose;) or in regard
of the parts themselves: as it is not possible
by the matter it selfe for any man, to determine how much more in this kinde may have
beene written by Antoninus; so if there were
never so much extant, yet how this that we
have here, could thereby be made more perfect
then it is, I doe not see. Their conceit, who
by reason of this undependance of matters,
would have the whole booke to be but excerpts
and Συλλογὰς of a greater, and better compacted worke; there being so many other
bookes both sacred and prophane written in
the same kinde; and Epictetus (the Patterne
of all latter Stoicks:) his Enchiridion among
the rest, it can at the best passe but for a meere
conceit, and needs I hope no other refutation.

To tell you then what I have done, and that
you may be the better satisfied that I except not
against Xylanders Interpretation without cause,
it remaines that for a specimen I produce some
few passages, by which it will be easie for any to
judge of the rest. But first I must faithfully
professe that my purpose in all this is not any
wayes to detract, either from Xylander himselfe,

or from the judgement of those learned men, by whom he hath beene highly commended, but rather to follow (after my best abilitie:) Xylanders owne example; whom for his great paines, and labour in his life-time to further and promote learning, I acknowledge to have deserved much honour and respect from all that love learning. I might adde that I shall deal with him more ingenuously too, then some others have done, who take upon them to correct some corrupt places of Antoninus, which Xylander in his Translation, whereof they take no notice, had already plainly corrected. But now to Antoninus.

Mistranslations

Where Antoninus in his first Booke saith, that hee learned by his Fathers example, that it is not impossible for a man that lives at the Court, (i. 17) ἐγγυτατω—δέοντα (read, νὴ Δία, ⟨μὴ διὰ⟩ τοῦτο). 'To live almost a private man's life, for matter of worldly pompe, and magnificence, and all outward shew and appearance (expressed by him before more at large:) and yet for all that, not to be a whit the more base and pusillanimous, or lesse stout or resolute in any publike affaires that shall require the power and authoritie of a Prince and Commander:' he translates it (Bas. edit. p. 174), *sed licere ei proximum privato homini habitum sumere: imò verò eum splendorem, eos qui principes rempublicam gerere velint, demissiores, segnioresque efficere.* Which neither of it selfe affords any tolerable sense, and is as wide from Antoninus his meaning, as any thing that could have beene conceived.

In the eight booke (Bas. edit. 247) Antoninus

PREFACE

Ant and Elephant alike perfect

saith that ἡ—ποιῆται: 'That the common Nature (which was one of the many Synonima's, by which the Stoicks did expresse God:) doth distribute all things in equalitie, as matter, forme, duration, and the like;' and then adds, σκόπει δὲ μὴ εἰ τὸ πρὸς τὸ ἓν ἴσον εὑρήσεις ἐπὶ παντός; 'This equalitie, thou shalt observe, not if absolutely thou shalt goe to compare all the particulars of any one thing by themselves, with the particulars of another by themselves:' ἀλλὰ—ἑτέρου (read τὰ πάντα τοῦδε), viii. 7; that is, 'But if thou consider all the particulars of any one thing together, with all the particulars of another, together likewise.' His meaning is, that every naturall thing in his owne kinde, that is, after a Geometricall, though not Arithmeticall equalitie, is equally perfect: an Ant, as perfect in her quantitie, as an Elephant and Whale, so great and vast, in theirs. As strong for her little proportion of body, and other circumstances of her nature, and as long lived, as any other creature; and so of all other things, if all things be well considered. And this doth not only extend to things of severall kinds and natures; but even to those that are of the same. It is a very pleasant and usefull speculation, as it may be prosecuted and applied, and it is very fully expressed by Antoninus. After this (as his manner is:) abruptly passing to another matter, Ἀναγιγνώσκειν οὐκ ἔξεστιν, saith he to himselfe (for so must the words be distinguished, which in the Greeke are viciously joyned and confounded—τὰ πάντα· τοῦ δὲ—ἀλλά, &c.) by way

of objection, and then immediately answers, **Love your enemies**
ἀλλὰ—ἔξεστιν, &c. 'Thou hast no time nor
opportunitie to reade bookes; What then?
Hast thou not time and opportunitie to practise
thy selfe not to doe any wrong:' (to thyselfe I
understand it; that is, to thy soule according to
Plato's doctrine, followed and expressed by
Antoninus, in those words at the beginning of
the second booke, ὕβριζε ὕβριζε ἑαυτὴν ὦ
ψυχή, &c., and againe at the end of the same
booke more at large:) 'to resist and overcome
all paines and pleasures, to contemne honour
and vaine glory, and not only not to be angry
with those whom thou dost find unsensible,
and unthankfull towards thee, but also to have
a care of them still, and of their welfare!' Conferre this with other like passages of Antoninus,
both for forme and matter, and you will thinke
that nothing could be plainer. (*See* v. 5, vii.
67), All this is expressed by Xylander: *Considera autem æqualitatem eam, inventurum te si
singulas res examines; sin unam cum universis
conferas, non item.* and then he leaves a blanck,
and beginnes a new line; *Atqui licet libidinem
arcere, voluptatibusque et doloribus superiorem
esse, itemque gloriola: licet etiam stupidis et ingratis non irasci.*

Some three or foure pages from the beginning
of the seventh Booke, τὸ ἐπίκοτον τοῦ προσώπου
(saith Antoninus:) λίαν—πρόσχημα ἢ (read εἰ)
τὸ—τοῦ ἁμαρτάνειν (read τοῦ μὴ ἁμαρτάνειν)
—αἰτία (vii. 24, Bas. edit. 234); "That an
angry countenance, (saith he) is much against

All passion is against reason

All nature, hence maist thou gather, because oftentimes it is the proper countenance of them that are at the point of death; and a forerunner of death as it were. But were it so that all anger and passion were so throughly quenched in thee, that it were altogether impossible that it should be kindled any more, yet herein must not thou rest satisfied, but further endeavour by good consequence of true ratiocination perfectly to conceive and understand, that all anger and passion is against reason: For if thou shalt not be sensible of thine innocencie, as it is innocencie; if that also shall bee gone from thee, the comfort of a good conscience, that thou doest all things to thy utmost power according to Reason, what shouldest thou desire to live any longer for?" (see iii. 6, xi. 14, viii. 2). All this is by Xylander contracted into these few words (page 251); *Irati vultus omnino est contra naturam, quando sæpius immoriendi sit prætextus, aut ad extremum extinctus est, ut omnino inflammari non potuerit. Hoc ipso intelligere labora, iram a ratione esse alienam. Nam si etiam sensus peccati nullus erit, quæ erit vivendi causa?*

At the end of the fift booke, Antoninus having spoken of some vanities, addes ἄνθρωπε—περισπούδαστα. 'O man hast thou forgotten what things these are? yea, but howsoever, they are things that other men much care for;' saith he, by way of objection; then answeres, διὰ τοῦτο—ποτέ· 'Wilt thou therefore be a foole also? it is enough that thou hast already beene one so long." And then passes to another matter: ὁπουδήποτε—πράξεις. "Let death surprise a man where and when it will. It is more then it can doe to make him therefore unhappy. He is an happy man, who (in his life time) dealeth unto himselfe a happy lot and portion. A happy lot and portion is, good inclinations of the soule; good motions, and desires, good actions." This passage cannot well bee translated, because wee have never a word answerable to the Greeke εὔμοιρος which Antoninus here elegantly, and acutely playes upon, which may signifie, either in generall a happy man, or in particular one that dyes happily: but properly signifies one that hath obtained a good part and portion. Howsoever, to render it as it may be rendred, the sense is very tolerable. Now Xylander having found the words somewhat confused, and incorrect, (for it is printed ἐγενόμην ποτέ ὁπουδήποτε καταλειφθεὶς εὔμοιρος ἄνθρωπος τὸ δὲ, etc.) translates them: *Propterea tu quoque stultus es factus? Aliquando utcunque relictus, factus sum fælix: Felicitas autem est, etc.*

At the end of the seventh Booke, Antoninus his words are, ἡ τοῦ ὅλου φύσις . . . ἤ τά λογικά (it is printed, ἤ ἀλόγιστα) καὶ . . . μνημονευόμενον. That the place must be so read and corrected (if any man make a question of it:) I will be judged by Antoninus himselfe vi. 44, vii. 73, not to mention others, as Arrianus lib. i., cap. 12, Ven. Edit., page 21. "The nature of the Universe," saith he, "did once

Errors corrected

Errors corrected certainely deliberate and resolve upon the creation of the world. What soever therefore, since that, is and happens in the world, is either but a consequent of that first, and one deliberation; (by which all things by a necessary and uninterrupted series of causes, were ordained and appointed to be:) or if so be that this Ruling rationall part of the world, takes any thought and care of things particular, They are surely his reasonable and principall creatures, that are the proper object of his particular care and providence. This often thought upon, will much conduce to thy tranquillitie." I take κυριώτατα here, as spoken of the same that λογικὰ; to which purpose he hath other passages, that reasonable creatures are the chiefest creatures. Yet if any man would rather have it; ἤ ἃ λογιστικὰ, τὰ κυριώτατα ἐστιν, ἐφ' ἃ, etc. 'reasonable creatures are his chiefest objects', I will not be against it, and it will be all one thing. But who could beare with Xylander his Interpretation, *Universi natura olim ad mundum fabricandum se contulit: nunc autem vel omnia quæ fiunt, consequentia fiunt sua: vel etiam in præcipuis eorum, ad quæ se mundi gubernatrix natura confert, rationi nullum locum esse et consilio, tenendum est. Hoc si memoria teneas, multis in rebus animo ut sis tranquilliori, efficiet.*

An easie matter it were to adde to these many more such passages, if I thought it as necessary, as it would be easie. They that shall take the paines (and it will be worth their paines I dare promise them) to compare diligently the Trans-

PREFACE

lations with Antoninus himselfe, will, I doubt not, before they have gone one or two Bookes over, be of my mind. I have of purpose made choice of such places especially, where I have made bold somewhat to correct the Text. I say bold, but no bolder I will maintain, then any reasonable man must, and ought, that doth undertake any such work. For I have not (to my knowledge :) by my Translation altered any one place in this kinde in the whole booke, but such as by certaine proofes and demonstrations from Antoninus himselfe, I can maintaine. Those places that I thought any thing doubtfull, I have given account of them to the Reader in my Notes. And if I have left any for desperate, as either imperfect or not intelligible by me, I may truly say, that had I taken to my selfe but the tenth part of the libertie, which Xylander doth usually throughout the whole book ; I needed not to have left any such places at all. And I make no question, but that in so doing, I might have given to many content and satisfaction good enough. But considering how much this libertie is commonly abused, and how prejudiciall it proves to good Authors, I have rather chosen sometimes to say lesse then I might, then to give unto others an example of this bold kinde of dealing with ancient Authors. The chiefest ground of all the obscurity in the Booke, is, that Antoninus having beene all his life an indefatigable student, and so read a world of writers of all sorts, his manner in these his bookes, as he read any thing that made for his

The Author's method

Quota- present purpose, closely and briefly to allude unto
tions in it, by some short meditation upon it: sometimes
the barely to excerpt some words, which either he
Medita- had an especiall liking unto, or afterward in-
tions tended further to meditate upon, without any
mention of the place or Author from whence
they are taken. Now many of these Authors
being quite perished, many of his allusions so
close and obscure, that though the Authors
be yet extant, yet it is not easie to finde from
whence, or of whom, nor to what intent or
purpose: it must not be wondred, if not only
many places seeme obscure, but some also of little
worth and use; because, it doth not appeare,
what further use Antoninus had of them in his
minde. Howsoever to them that are any thing
versed in the writings of ancient Philosophers,
Stoicks especially, there will not occurre many
such places. If a man take but Arrianus, and
Seneca, and compare them diligently with Antoninus, he will finde a marvellous consent, and
many obscure short places of Antoninus, illus-
trated and explained by their larger discourse.
I have done it in some few places, which I
thought could not well otherwise be understood.
And for the rest, I leave them to every diligent
Readers industrie. Neither indeed would I
have put my selfe to the labour of writing any
Notes at all, if the booke could as well have
wanted them, as I could easilie have found as
well, or better to my minde, how to bestow my
time. However as I thought some would be
needfull, so did I thinke also, that if in the former

Bookes, I did give satisfaction to the Reader, I might afterwards be spared, and either be trusted my selfe, or trust to the Readers diligence and abilitie for the rest. Wheresoever by supplying a word or two in the Text, I thought I could helpe the sense, and illustrate the matter sufficiently; to spare my selfe a Note, and for the case of the Reader, I have done it. And whereas those former passages by me produced wherein I except against the Latine Translation, are all such as could not be well translated without some correction of the Text, that it may not bee thought, that in such places only it is amisse, I have for the further satisfaction of the Reader (the bookes as hath already been said, being so scarce and hard to be come by:) taken occasion in my Notes, now and then to instance in some other passages, wherein there can be no such exception. In the Author himselfe I feare exception will be taken, at many places, as meere repetitions; at some others, wherein he seemeth to contradict what hee had said before. But if the Readers consider, first, that what Antoninus wrote, he wrote it not for the publick, but for his owne private use; and secondly, that Antoninus his words are so intermingled every where with his *Excerpta*, that it doth not well appeare what is his owne, and what is not; as in regard of the first consideration they will, I doubt not, allow him farre more libertie than otherwise were fitting: so in regard of the second, I presume they will yeeld both those many suspected repetitions in the Bookes, and those few supposed

Repetitions and Contradictions

PREFACE

How a Christian should read the Book

contradictions, the one perchance to be but severall collections of one subject and to one purpose from severall Authors; and the others certainely, rather the different opinions of different Authors concerning the same thing, then the contradictions of one man, inconstant to himselfe. And as for such places which may give offence, as repugnant to our Christian faith, and impious; as when hee seemeth to speake doubtfully of God, and his Providence; and to adscribe all things to Fatall necessity, and the like: I shall but desire the Readers to remember who hee was that wrote, and I hope they will desire no other satisfaction in this point. For that any Christian should expect from any out of the Church and without the Scriptures perfect sound knowledge in these high points would be no small wonder to mee: it being both the happinesse of every the meanest Christian, that he may know more in these mysteries, then the greatest Philosophers could ever, with all their wit and learning, attaine unto; and the proper priviledge of the divine Scriptures, that from them only all solid truth in points of this nature, is to be expected. However that Antoninus may not want any just defence that his cause doth afford, the Reader must further be intreated not to judge of his opinions, by one or two short passages here and there, occurrent, which whether they be his or no (as we have already said) is hard to determine; but to have a respect to other more large, and peremptory passages concerning the same purpose elsewhere to be found. As for example concerning God and his Providence, to B. ii. Num. 11, B. vi. Num. 44, &c., and concerning Fatall necessitie not only to the same Lib. ii. Num. 11 but also to divers other places, as B. viii. Num. 7, 29, 32, 34, 48, &c., by which places as it doth plainly appeare, that he doth exclude all manner of Necessitie from humane wils and actions, so doth it appeare by other passages, as Lib. viii. Num. 35, that he did not altogether exclude from all divine providence not even those actions of men, that are most contrary to the will of God: from which place moreover may appeare what it is that he often calls εἱμαρμένην, Fate, or Destinie; which in his meaning is no other then (as by divers other Philosophers also it is expounded) Gods order and providence in matters of the world: to which purpose hee doth also expound the word Fortune, B. i. Num. 17. On the other side, although he doth every where very absolutely maintaine this libertie of mans will, and that he was not acquainted with the mysterie of originall sinne, and naturall concupiscence; yet shall you not finde in him those blasphemies, in exaltation of this humane power and libertie, which you shall in Seneca, and other Stoicks: neither did he (it should seeme, though but an Heathen:) so much rely upon it, **but** that he doth very piously commend prayers, as very powerfull and effectuall unto vertue. See lib. ix. Num. 40. Now if Antoninus himselfe being a Romane, for the propriety and facilitie of his expressions (wherein the Latine

Antoninus' views

PREFACE

Antoninus' care in composing

tongue, in matter of Philosophie, comes as short of the Greeke, as the English doth of the Latine:) did in the composing of these his Bookes preferre the Greeke tongue before his owne mother tongue; no man I hope will expect, that all things should in this Translation runne so smoothly, as in another kinde of Translation happily they might. But herein I must confesse my feare is for Antoninus, more then for my selfe. For first whereas he, being (I thinke) as well acquainted with ancient writers and philosophers as ever any was, doth every where very strictly and carefully observe their proper choise words and termes, which both make the sense it selfe more current, and pleasing; and for a Scholler to know them and to be acquainted with them, is in many respects very usefull; This in the Translation must needs be lost, and by consequent so much lost to Antoninus, of his due praise and commendation. And secondly, whereas in all these his 12 bookes there be not many lines (if any:) which if well considered, will not be found either to be taken out of some ancient Author, or at least by way either of Exception, Confirmation, Illustration, and the like, to either passage or opinion of some ancient to have some relation; as to Schollars I know whatsoever is in this kinde, be it otherwise what it will, cannot but bee acceptable and usefull, so to others I feare, many things for want of this use of it which they are not capable of, will seeme but drie and impertinent. In these two respects I cannot deny but I have done Antoninus some wrong to Thanks make him so vulgar, as I have done, and yet rendered because I thought hee might in other respects doe good to any that should read him, if before the credit of one I have preferred the good of many, I have but done what Antoninus himselfe (as by these his bookes may appeare:) would have me or any others doe in the like case.

And now in the last place, if any shall by these my paines receive any content, my desire is that they would thanke him, by whose encouragement especially I did undertake this little worke, my Reverend Kinde friend Dr Lyndsell, the right worthy Bishop of Peter-borough, a man for his singular worth and learning in all kinde of literature, not to be named by any that know Him, without expression of all due respect and admiration; and one to whom my selfe, and my studies of old have beene much beholding, as I shall ever most gladly acknowledge.

M. AUREL. ANTONINUS THE ROMANE EMPEROUR, HIS FIRST BOOKE

concerning HIMSELF:

Wherein Antoninus recordeth, What and of whom, whether Parents, Friends, or Masters; by their good examples, or good advice and counsell, he had learned:

Divided into Numbers or Sections.

ANTONINUS Booke vi. Num. xlviii. Whensoever thou wilt rejoyce thy selfe, thinke and meditate upon those good parts and especiall gifts, which thou hast observed in any of them that live with thee: as industrie in one, in another modestie, in another bountifulnesse, in another some other thing. For nothing can so much rejoyce thee, as the resemblances and parallels of several vertues, eminent in the dispositions of them that live with thee, especially when all at once, as it were, they represent themselves unto thee. See therefore, that thou have them alwayes in a readinesse.

Num. I.

OF my Grandfather Verus I have learned to bee gentle and meeke, and to refraine from all anger and passion. From the fame and memory of him that begot mee I have learned both shamefastnesse and manlike behaviour. Of my Mother I have learned to be religious, and bountifull; and to forbeare, not only to doe, but

Inherited qualities

The Author's debt to Diognetus

to intend any evill; to content my selfe with a spare dyet, and to fly all such excesse as is incidentall to great wealth. Of my great Grandfather, both to frequent publike schooles and Auditories, and to get me good and able Teachers at home; and that I ought not to think much, if upon such occasions, I were at excessive charges.

II. Of him that brought mee up, not to be fondly addicted to either of the two great factions of the coursers in the Circus, called Prasini, and Veneti: nor in the Amphitheater partially to favour any of the Gladiators, or fencers, as either the Parmularii, or the Secutoriani. Moreover, to endure labour; not to need many things; when I have any thing to doe, to doe it my selfe rather then by others; not to meddle with many businesses; and not easily to admit of any slander.

III. Of Diognetus, not to busie my selfe about vaine things, and not easily to beleeve those things, which are commonly spoken, by such as take upon them to worke wonders, and by Sorcerers, or, praestigiators, and impostors; concerning the power of charmes, and their driving out of Dæmons, or evill spirits; and the like. Not to keep coturnices, or quailes for the game; nor to bee mad after such things. Not to be offended with other mens liberty of speech, and to apply my selfe unto Philosophy. Him also I must thanke, that ever I heard first Bacchius, then Tandasis and Marcianus, and that I did write Dialogues in my youth; and that I tooke liking to the Philosophers little couch and to and skins, and such other things, which by the Rusticus Græcian discipline are proper to those who professe philosophie.

IV. To Rusticus I am beholding, that I first entred into the conceit that my life wanted some redresse, and cure. And then, that I did not fall into the ambition of ordinary Sophists, either to write tracts concerning the common Theorems, or to exhort men unto vertue and the study of philosophie by publike orations; as also that I never by way of ostentation did affect to shew my selfe an active able man, for any kinde of bodily exercises. And that I gave over the studie of Rhetorick and Poetry, and of elegant neate language. That I did not use to walke about the house in my long robe, nor to doe any such things. Moreover I learned of him to write letters without any affectation, or curiosity; such as that was, which by him was written to my Mother from Sinoessa: and to be easie and ready to be reconciled, and well pleased againe with them that had offended mee, as soone as any of them would be content to seeke unto me againe. To read with diligence; not to rest satisfied with a light and superficiall knowledge, nor quickly to assent to things commonly spoken of: whom also I must thanke that ever I lighted upon Epictetus his Hypomnemata, or morall commentaries and commonefactions: which also hee gave me of his owne.

V. From Apollonius, true liberty, and unvariable stedfastnesse, and not to regard any

How to be both vehement and remiss thing at all, though never so little, but right and reason: and alwayes, whether in the sharpest paines, or after the losse of a child, or in long diseases, to be still the same man; who also was a present and visible example unto mee, that it was possible for the same man to be both vehement and remisse: a man not subject to be vexed, and offended with the incapacitie of his Scholars and Auditors in his lectures and expositions; and a true patterne of a man who of all his good gifts and faculties, least esteemed in himselfe, that his excellent skill and abilitie to teach and perswade others the common Theorems, and Maxims of the Stoick Philosophie. Of him also I learned how to receive favours and kindnesses (as commonly they are accounted:) from friends, so that I might not become obnoxious unto them, for them, nor more yeelding upon occasion, then in right I ought; and yet so that I should not passe them neither, as an unsensible and unthankfull man.

VI. Of Sextus, mildnesse and the patterne of a family governed with paternall affection; and a purpose to live according to nature: to be grave without affectation: to observe carefully the severall dispositions of my friends, not to be offended with Idiots, nor unseasonably to set upon those that are carryed with the vulgar opinions, with the Theorems, and Tenets of Philosophers: his conversation being an example how a man might accommodate himselfe to all men and companies; so that though his company were sweeter and more pleasing, then any

flatterers cogging and fauning; **yet** was it at the Polite
same time most respected and reverenced: who correction
also had a proper happinesse, and facultie, ration-
ally, and methodically to finde out, and set in
order all necessary Dogmata, or determinations
and instructions for a mans life. A man without ever the least appearance of anger, or any
other passion; able at the same time most
exactly to observe the stoick Apathia, or
unpassionatnesse, and yet to be most tender
hearted: ever of good credit; and yet almost
without any noise, or rumor: very learned, and
yet making little shew.

VII. From Alexander the Grammarian, to
be unreproveable my selfe, and not reproachfully
to reprehend any man for a barbarisme, or a
soloecisme, or any false pronunciation, but dex-
trously by way of answere, or testimonie, or
confirmation of the same matter (taking no
notice of the word) to utter it as it should
have beene spoken; or by some other such
close and indirect admonition, handsomely **and**
civilly to tell him of it.

VIII. Of Fronto, to how much envy and
fraud, and hypocrisie the state of a Tyrannous
King is subject unto, and how they who are
commonly called εὐπατρίδαι or patricii, i. nobly
borne, are in some sort incapable, or voide of
naturall affection.

IX. Of Alexander the Platonick, not often
nor without great necessity to say, or to write
to any man in a letter, I am not at leasure;
nor in this manner still to put off those duties,

An equal common-wealth which **wee owe to our** friends and acquaintances, (to every one in his kinde) under pretence of urgent affaires.

X. Of Catulus, not to contemne any friends expostulation, though unjust, but to strive to reduce him to his former disposition: Freely and heartily to speake well of all my Masters upon any occasion, as it is reported of Domitius, and Athenodotus, and to love my children with true affection.

XI. From my Brother Severus, to be kind and loving to all them of my house and family; by whom also I came to the knowledge of Thrasea and Helvidius, and Cato, and Dio, and Brutus. He it was also that did put me in the first conceit and desire of an equall common wealth, administred by Justice and equality; and of a Kingdome wherein should be regarded nothing more then the good and welfare of the subjects. Of him also, to observe a constant tenour, (not interrupted, with any other **cares** and distractions,) in the studie and esteeme of Philosophy: **to** bee bountifull and liberall in the largest measure; alwayes to hope the best; and to be confident that my friends love me. In whom I moreover observed open dealing towards those whom he reproved at any time, and that his friends might without all doubt or much observation know what he would, or would not, **so** open and plaine was hee.

XII. From Claudius Maximus, in all things to endeavour to have power of my selfe, and in nothing to be carryed about; to bee cheerefull

and couragious in all suddaine chances and acci- **The**
dents, as in sicknesses: to love mildnesse, and **Author's**
moderation, and gravitie: and to do my busines, **Father**
whatsoever it be, thorowly, and without querelousnesse. Whatsoever he said, all men beleeved him that as he spake, so he thought, and whatsoever he did, that he did it with a good intent. His manner was, never to wonder at any thing; never to be in hast, and yet never slow: nor to be perplexed, or dejected, or at any time unseemely, or excessively to laugh: nor to be angry, or suspicious, but ever ready to doe good, and to forgive, and to speake truth; and all this, as one that seemed rather of himselfe to have been straight and right, then ever to have beene rectified, or redressed: neither was there any man that ever thought himselfe undervalued by him, or that could finde in his heart, to thinke himselfe a better man then he. He would also be very pleasant and gracious.

XIII. In my Father, I observed his meeknesse; his constancie without wavering in those things, which after a due examination and deliberation, he had determined. How free from all vanity he carried himselfe in matter of honour and dignitie, (as they are esteemed:) his laboriousnesse, and assiduitie, his readinesse to heare any man, that had ought to say, tending to any common good: how generally and impartially he would give every man his due; his skill and knowledge, when rigour or extremity, or when remisnesse or moderation was in season; how he did abstaine from all unchast love of youths; his

D

His care, cheerful-ness, sobriety moderate condescending to other mens occasions as an ordinary man, neither absolutely requiring of his friends, that they should waite upon him at his ordinary meales, nor that they should of necessity accompany him in his journies; and that whensoever any businesse upon some necessary occasions was to be put off and omitted before it could be ended, he was ever found when he went about it againe, the same man that he was before. His accurate examination of things in consultations, and patient hearing of others. He would not hastily give over the search of the matter, as one easie to be satisfied with suddaine notions and apprehensions. His care to preserve his friends; how neither at any time hee would carry himselfe towards them with disdainfull neglect, and grow weary of them; nor yet at any time bee madly fond of them. His contented minde in all things, his chearefull countenance, his care to foresee things afarre off, and to take order for the least, without any noise or clamour. Moreover, how all acclamations and flattery were repressed by him: how carefully hee observed all things necessary to the government, and kept an account of the common expences, and how patiently he did abide that he was reprehended by some for this his strict and rigid kind of dealing. How hee was neither a superstitious worshipper of the gods, nor an ambitious pleaser of men, or studious of popular applause; but sober in all things, and every where observant of that which was fitting; no affecter of novelties: in those things which conduced to his ease and convenience, (plenty whereof his fortune did afford him,) without pride and bragging, yet with all freedome and libertie: so that as he did freely enjoy them without any anxiety or affectation when they were present; so when absent, he found no want of them. Moreover, that he was never commended by any man, as either a learned acute man, or an obsequious officious man, or a fine Oratour; but as a ripe mature man, a perfect sound man; one that could not endure to be flattered; able to governe both himselfe and others. Moreover, how much he did honour all true philosophers, without upbraiding those that were not so; his sociablenesse, his gracious and delightfull conversation, but never unto satiety; his care of his body within bounds and measure, not as one that desired to live long, or over-studious of neatnesse, and elegancie; and yet not as one that did not regard it: so that through his owne care and providence, hee seldome needed any inward Physick, or outward applications: but especially how ingeniously he would yeeld to any that had obtained any peculiar faculty, as either Eloquence, or the knowledge of the lawes, or of ancient customs, or the like; and how he concurred with them, in his best care and endeavour that every one of them might in his kinde, for that wherein he excelled, be regarded and esteemed: and although hee did all things carefully after the ancient customes of his forefathers, yet even of this was he not

A ripe mature man

His dis- desirous that men should take notice, that hee
cretion did imitate ancient customes. Againe, how he
and was not easily moved and tossed up and downe,
modera-
 tion but loved to be constant, both in the same
places and businesses; and how after his great
fits of head-ach, he would returne fresh and
vigorous to his wonted affaires. Againe, that
secrets he neither had many, nor often, and
such only as concerned publike matters: His
discretion and moderation, in exhibiting of the
Spectacula, or, publike sights and showes for
the pleasure and pastime of the people: in
publicke buildings, Congiaries, and the like.
In all these things, having a respect unto men
only as men, and to the equity of the things
themselves, and not unto the glory that might
follow. Never wont to use the baths at unseasonable houres; no builder; never curious,
or solicitous, either about his meat, or about
the workmanship, or colour of his clothes,
or about any thing that belonged to externall
beauty. . . . In all his conversation, farre
from all inhumanity, all boldnesse, and incivi-
ilitie, all greedinesse and impetuositie; never
doing anything with such earnestnesse, and intention, that a man could say of him, that
hee did sweat about it: but contrariwise, all
things distinctly, as at leasure; without trouble;
orderly, soundly, and agreeably. A man might
have applyed that to him, which is recorded
of Socrates, that he knew how to want, and
to enjoy those things, in the want whereof,
most men shew themselves weake; and in the

fruition, intemperate: But to hold out firme and constant, and to keepe within the compasse of true moderation and sobriety in either estate, is proper to a man, who hath a perfect and invincible soule; such as he shewed himselfe in the sicknesse of Maximus.

A Prince may live without state

XIV. From the gods I received that **I had** good Grandfathers, and Parents, a good Sister, good masters, good domesticks, loving kinsmen, almost all that I have; and that I never through hast, and rashnesse transgressed against any of them, notwithstanding that my disposition was such, as that such a thing (if occasion had beene) might very well have beene committed by me, but that it was the mercy of the gods, **to** prevent such a concurring of matters and occasions, as might make mee to incurre this blame. That I was not long brought up by the Concubine of my Father; that I preserved the flower of my youth. That I tooke not upon me to be a man before my time, but rather put it off longer then I needed. That I lived under the government of my Lord and Father, who would take away from me all pride and vaine-glory, and reduce me to that conceit and opinion that it was not impossible for a Prince to live in the Court without a troope of guards and followers, extraordinary apparell, such and such torches and statues, and other like particulars of state and magnificence; but that a man may reduce and contract himselfe almost to the state of a private man, and yet for all that not to become the more base and remisse in those publick matters and affaires,

The good gifts of the Gods wherein power and authority is requisite. That I have had such a Brother, who by his owne example might stirre me up to thinke of my selfe; and by his respect and love, delight and please me. That I have got ingenuous children, and that they were not borne distorted, nor with any other naturall deformity. That I was no great proficient in the study of Rhetorick and Poetry, and of other faculties, which perchance I might have dwelt upon, if I had found myselfe to goe on in them with successe. That I did by times preferre those, by whom I was brought up, to such places and dignities, which they seemed unto me most to desire; and that I did not put them off with hope and expectation, that (since that they were yet but young) I would doe the same hereafter. That I ever knew Apollonius and Rusticus, and Maximus. That I have had occasion often and effectually to consider and meditate with my selfe, concerning that life which is according to nature, what the nature and manner of it is: So that as for the gods and such suggestions, helpes and inspirations, as might be expected from them, nothing did hinder, but **that I** might have begunne long before to live according to nature; or that even now that I was not yet partaker and in present possession of that life, that I my selfe (in that I did not observe those inward motions, and suggestions, yea and almost plaine and apparant instructions and admonitions of the gods,) was the only cause of it. That my body in such a life, hath beene able to hold out so long. That I never had to doe with Benedicta and Theodotus, yea and afterwards when I *A blame-* fell into some fits of love, I was soone cured. *less life* That having beene often displeased with Rusticus, I never did him any thing, for which afterwards I had occasion to repent. That it being so that my Mother was to die young, yet shee **lived** with me all her latter yeares. That as often as I had a purpose to helpe and succour any that either was poor, or fallen into some present necessity, I never was answered by my Officers that there was not ready money enough to doe it ; and that I my selfe never had occasion to require the like succour from any other. That I have such a wife, so obedient, so loving, so ingenuous. That I had choice of fit and able men, to whom I might commit the bringing up of my children. That by dreames I have received helpe, as for other things, so in particular, how I might stay my casting of blood, and cure my dizzenesse, as that also that hapned to thee in Cajeta, as unto Chryses when he prayed by the sea-shore. And when I did first apply my selfe to Philosophie, that I did not fall into the hands of some sophists, or spent my time either in reading the manifold volumes of ordinary philosophers, nor in practising my selfe in the solution of arguments and fallacies, nor dwelt upon the studies of the Metheores, and other naturall curiosities. All these things without the assistance of the gods, and fortune, could not have beene.

XV. In the Countrey of the Quadi at Granua, these.

Betimes in the morning say to thy selfe, This

Brotherly charity to all men day I shall have to doe with an idle curious man, with an unthankfull man, a railer, a crafty, false, or an envious man; an unsociable uncharitable man. All these ill qualities have hapned unto them, through ignorance of that which is truly good and truly bad. But I that understand the nature of that which is good, that it onely is to be desired, and of that which is bad, that it onely is truly odious and shameful: who know moreover, that this transgressor, whosoever he be, is my kinsman, not by the same blood and seed, but by participation of the same reason, and of the same divine particle; How can I either be hurt by any of those, since it is not in their power to make me incurre anything that is truly reproachfull? or angry, and ill affected towards him, who by nature is so neere unto me? for we are all borne to bee fellow workers, as the feet, the hands, and the eye-lids; as the rowes of the upper and under teeth: for such therefore to be in opposition, is against nature; and what is it to chafe at, and to be averse from, but to be in opposition?

XVI. Whatsoever I am, is either flesh, or life, or that which wee commonly call the mistris and over-ruling part of man; reason. Away with thy bookes, suffer not thy minde any more to be distracted, and carryed to and fro; for it will not be; but as even now readie to die, thinke little of thy flesh: blood, bones, and a skin; a pretty piece of knit and twisted worke, consisting of nerves, veines and arteries; thinke no more of it, then so. And as for thy life,

consider what it is; a winde; not one constant **Thou art**
winde neither, but every moment of an houre let **a part of**
out, and suckt in againe. The third, is thy **the whole**
ruling part; and here consider; Thou art an old
man; suffer not that excellent part to bee brought
in subjection, and to become slavish: suffer it not
to be drawne up and downe with unreasonable
and unsociable lusts and motions, as it were with
wyres and nerves; suffer it not any more, either
to repine at any thing now present, or to feare and
fly any thing to come, which the Destinie hath
appointed thee.

XVII. Whatsoever proceeds from the gods
immediately, that any man will grant totally
depends from their divine providence. As for
those things that are commonly said to happen
by Fortune, even those must be conceived to
have dependance from nature, or from that first
and generall connexion, and concatenation of all
those things, which more apparantly by the
divine providence are administred and brought
to passe. All things flow from thence: And
whatsoever it is that is, is both necessary, and
conducing to the whole; part of which thou art:
and whatsoever it is that is requisite and necessary for the preservation of the generall, must of
necessity for every particular nature, bee good
and behoovefull. And as for the whole, it is preserved, as by the perpetuall mutation and conversion of the simple Elements one into another, so
also by the mutation, and alteration of things
mixed and compounded. Let these things
suffice thee; Let them be alwayes unto thee, as

<small>Go about each action as if thy last</small> thy generall rules and precepts. As for thy thirst after bookes, away with it with all speed that thou die not murmuring and complaining, but truly meeke and well satisfied, and from thy heart thankfull unto the gods.

The Second Booke

REMEMBER how long thou hast already put off these things, and how often a certaine day and houre as it were, having been set unto thee by the gods, thou hast neglected it. It is high time for thee to understand the true nature both of the world, whereof thou art a part; and of that Lord and Governour of the World, from whom, as a channell from the spring, thou thy selfe didst flow: And that there is but a certaine limit of time appointed unto thee, which if thou shalt not make use of to calme and alay the many distempers of thy soule, it will passe away and thou with it, and never after returne.

II. Let it be thy earnest and incessant care as a Romane and a man to performe whatsoever it is that thou art about, with true and unfained gravity, naturall affection, freedome and justice: and as for all other cares, and imaginations, how thou mayest ease thy minde of them. Which thou shalt doe; if thou shalt goe about every action as thy last action, free from all vanitie, all passionate and wilfull aberration from reason, and from all hypocrisie, and selfe-love, and dislike of those things, which by the fates, or appointment of God have hapned unto thee. Thou seest that those things, which for a man to hold on in a prosperous course, and to live a divine life, are requisite and necessary, are not many, for the gods will require no more of any man, that shall but keepe and observe these things.

Man's happiness depends from himself

III. Doe, Soule, doe; abuse and contemne thy selfe; yet a while and the time for thee to respect thy selfe, will be at an end. Every mans happinesse depends from himselfe, but behold thy life is almost at an end, whiles affording thy selfe no respect, thou dost make thy happinesse to consist in the soules, and conceits of other men.

IV. Why should any of these things that happen externally, so much distract thee? Give thy selfe leisure to learne some good thing, and cease roving and wandring to and fro. Thou must also take heed of another kinde of wandring, for they are idle in their actions, who toile and labour in this life, and have no certaine scope to which to direct all their motions, and desires.

V. For not observing the state of another mans soule, scarce was ever any man knowne to be unhappy. But whosoever they be that intend not, and guide not by reason and discretion the motions of their owne soules, they must of necessity be unhappy.

VI. These things thou must alwayes have in minde: What is the nature of the Universe, and what is mine in particular: This unto that what relation it hath: what kinde of part, of what kinde of Universe it is: And that there is

The gods will do thee no hurt no body that can hinder thee, but that thou mayest alwayes, both doe and speake those things which are agreeable to that Nature whereof thou art a part.

VII. Theophrastus, where he compares sinne with sinne (as after a vulgar sense such things I grant may be compared:) sayes well and like a philosopher, that those sinnes are greater which are committed through lust, then those which are committed through anger. For he that is angry seemes with a kinde of griefe and close contraction of himselfe, to turne away from reason; but he that sinnes through lust, being overcome by pleasure, doth in his very sin bewray a more impotent, and unmanlike disposition. Well then and like a philosopher doth he say, that he of the two is the more to be condemned, that sins with pleasure, then he that sinnes with griefe. For indeed this latter may seeme first to have beene wronged, and so in some manner through griefe thereof to have been forced to be angry, whereas he who through lust doth commit any thing, did of himselfe meerly resolve upon that action.

VIII. Whatsoever thou doest affect, whatsoever thou doest project, so doe, and so project all, as one who, for ought thou knowest, may at this very present depart out of this life. And as for death, if there be any gods, it is no grievous thing to leave the society of men. The gods will doe thee no hurt thou maist be sure. But if it be so that there be no gods, or that they take no care of the world, why should I desire to live in a world void of gods, and of all divine providence? But gods there be certainely, and they take care for the world; and as for those things which be truly evill, as vice and wickednesse, such things they have put in a mans owne power, that he might avoid them if he would: and had there beene any thing besides that had been truly bad and evill, they would have had a care of that also, that a man might have avoided it. But why should that be thought to hurt and prejudice a mans life in this world, which cannot any wayes make man himselfe the better, or the worse in his owne person? Neither must wee thinke that the Nature of the Universe did either through ignorance passe these things, or if not as ignorant of them, yet as unable either to prevent, or better to order and dispose them. It cannot be that shee through want either of power or skill, should have committed such a thing, so as to suffer all things both good and bad, equally and promiscuously to happen unto all both good and bad. As for life therefore, and death, honour and dishonour, labour and pleasure, riches and poverty, all these things happen unto men indeed, both good and bad, equally; but as things which of themselves are neither good nor bad; because of themselves, neither shamefull nor praise-worthy.

IX. Consider how quickly all things are dissolved and resolved: the bodyes and substances themselves, into the matter and substance of the world: and their memories into the generall Age and Time of the world. Consider the nature of all worldly sensible things; of those

What is it to die? especially, which either insnare by pleasure, or for their irkesomenesse are dreadfull, or for their outward luster and shew are in great esteeme and request, how vile and contemptible, how base and corruptible, how destitute of all true life and being they are.

X. It is the part of a man endowed with a good understanding facultie, to consider what they themselves are in very deed, from whose bare conceits and voices, honour and credit doe proceed: as also what it is to die, and how if a man shall consider this by it selfe alone, to die, and separate from it in his minde all those things which with it usually represent themselves unto us, he can conceive of it no otherwise, then as of a worke of nature, and he that feares any worke of nature, is a very child. Now death, it is not only a worke of Nature, but also conducing to Nature.

XI. Consider with thy selfe how man, and by what part of his, is joyned unto God, and how that part of man is affected, when it is said to be diffused. There is nothing more wretched then that soule, which in a kinde of circuit compasseth all things, searching (as he saith) even the very depths of the Earth; and by all signes and conjectures prying into the very thoughts of other mens soules; and yet of this is not sensible, that it is sufficient for a man to apply himselfe wholly, and to confine all his thoughts and cares to the tendance of that Spirit, which is within him, and truly and really to serve him. His service doth consist in this, that a man keepe him-

selfe pure from all violent passion, and evill affec- **To lose**
tion, from all rashnesse and vanity, and from all **but the**
manner of discontent, either in regard of the **flying**
gods, or men. For indeed whatsoever proceeds **moment**
from the gods, deserves respect for their worth
and excellencie; and whatsoever proceeds from
men, as they are our kinsmen, should by us be
entertained, with love, alwayes; sometimes, as
proceeding from their ignorance of that which
is truly good and bad, (a blindnesse no lesse,
then that by which wee are not able to discerne
betweene white and black:) with a kinde of
pitty and compassion also.

XII. If thou shouldst live 3000, or as many
10,000 of yeares, yet remember this, that man
can part with no life properly, save with that
little part of life, which hee now lives: and that
which he lives, is no other, then that which at
every instant he parts with. That then which is
longest of duration, and that which is shortest,
come both to one effect. For although in regard
of that which is already past there may be some
inequalitie, yet that time which is now present
and in being, is equall unto all men. And that
being it which wee part with whensoever we die,
it doth manifestly appeare, that it can bee but a
moment of time, that wee then part with. For
as for that which is either past or to come, a
man cannot be said properly to part with it. For
how should a man part with that which he hath
not? These two things therefore thou must remember. First, that all things in the world from
all eternitie, by a perpetuall revolution of the

All is opinion same times and things ever continued and renued, are of one kinde and nature; so that whether for a 100 or 200 hundred yeares onely, or for an infinite space of time, a man see those things which are still the same, it can be no matter of great moment. And secondly, that that life which any the longest liver, or the shortest liver parts with, is for length and duration the very same, for that only which is present, is that, which either of them can lose, as being that only which they have, for that which he hath not, no man can truly be said to lose.

XIII. Remember that all is but opinion and conceit, for those things are plaine and apparant, which were spoken unto Monimus the Cynick, and as plaine and apparant is the use that may be made of those things, if that which is true and serious in them, be received as well as that which is sweet and pleasing.

XIV. A mans soule doth wrong and disrespect it selfe first and especially, when as much as in it selfe lyes it becomes an Aposteme, and as it were an excrescencie of the world, for to be grieved and displeased with any thing that happens in the world, is direct apostasie from the Nature of the Universe; part of which, all particular Natures of the world, are: Secondly, when shee either is averse from any man, or lead by contrary desires and affections, tending to his hurt and prejudice; such as are the soules of them that are angry. Thirdly, when shee is overcome by any pleasure or paine. Fourthly, when shee doth dissemble, and covertly and falsely, either doth or saith any thing. Fiftly, when shee doth **Life is a** either affect or endeavour any thing to no certain **pilgrim-** end, but rashly and without due ratiocination, **age** and consideration, how consequent or inconsequent it is to the common end. For even the least things ought not to be done, without relation unto the end ; and the end of the reasonable creatures is, to follow and obey him, who is the reason as it were, and the law of this great City, and ancient Common-wealth.

XV. The time of a mans life is as a point ; the substance of it ever flowing, the sense obscure ; and the whole composition of the body, tending to corruption. His soule is restlesse, fortune uncertaine, and fame doubtfull : to be briefe, as a streame so are all things belonging to the body ; as a dreame, or as a smoake, so are all that belong unto the soule. Our life is a warfare, and a meere pilgrimage. Fame after life, is no better than oblivion. What is it then that will adhere and follow ? Only one thing, Philosophy. And philosophie doth consist in this, for a man to preserve that Spirit which is within him, from all manner of contumelies and injuries, and above all paines or pleasures ; never to doe any thing either rashly, or fainedly, or hypocritically : wholly to depend from himselfe, and his owne proper actions : all things that happen unto him to embrace contentedly, as comming from Him from whom He Himselfe also came ; and above all things, with all meeknesse and a calme chearfulnesse, to expect death, as being nothing else, but the resolution of those Elements, of which

How to use Life every creature is composed. And if the Elements themselves suffer nothing by this **their** perpetuall conversion of one into another, that dissolution, and alteration, which is so common unto all, why should it be feared by any? Is not this according to nature? But nothing that is according to Nature, can be evill.

Whilest I was at Carnuntum.

The Third Booke

A MAN must not only consider how daily his life wasteth and decreaseth, but this also, that if he live long, hee cannot be certaine, whether his understanding shall continue so able and sufficient, for either discreet consideration, in matter of businesses; or for contemplation: it being the thing, whereon true knowledge of things both divine and humane, doth depend. For if once he shall beginne to dote, his respiration, nutrition, his imaginative, and appetitive, and other naturall faculties, may still continue the same: he shall finde no want of them. But how to make that right use of himselfe that he should, how to observe exactly in all things that which is right and just, how to redresse and rectifie all wrong, or suddaine apprehensions and imaginations, and even of this particular, whether he should live any longer or no, to consider duly; for all such things, wherein the best strength, and vigour of the minde is most re-

quisite; his power and abilitie will be passed **Beauty**
and gone. Thou must hasten therefore; not **in natural**
only because thou art every day neerer unto **processes**
death then other, but also because that intellective facultie in thee, whereby thou art inabled
to know the true nature of things, and to order
all thy actions by that knowledge, doth daily
wast and decay: or, may faile thee before thou
die.

II. This also thou must observe, that whatsoever it is that naturally doth happen to things
naturall, hath somewhat in it selfe, that is pleasing and delightfull, as a great loafe when it is
baked, some parts of it cleave as it were, and
part asunder, and make the crust of it rugged
and unequall, and yet those parts of it, though in
some sort it be against the art and intention of
baking it selfe, that they are thus cleft and parted,
which should have beene, and were first made all
even and uniforme, they become it well neverthelesse, and have a certaine peculiar property, to
stirre the appetite. So figs are accounted fairest
and ripest then, when they beginne to shrinke,
and wither as it were. So ripe olives, when
they are next to putrefaction, then are they in
their proper beautie. The hanging downe of
grapes, the brow of a Lyon; the froath of a
foaming wilde boare, and many other like things,
though by themselves considered, they are farre
from any beautie, yet because they happen
naturally, they both are comely, and delightfull; so that if a man shall with a profound
minde and apprehension, consider all things in

Beauty of old age the world, even among all those things which are but meere accessories, and naturall appendices as it were, there will scarce appeare any thing unto him, wherein he will not finde matter of pleasure and delight. So will he behold with as much pleasure the true *rictus* of wilde beasts, as those which by skilfull painters, and other artificers are imitated. So will he bee able to perceive the proper ripenesse and beauty of old age, whether in man, or woman: and whatsoever else it is that is beautifull and alluring in whatsoever is, with chast and continent eyes, he will soone finde out and discerne. Those and many other things will he discerne, not credible unto every one, but unto them only who are truly and familiarly acquainted, both with nature it selfe, and all naturall things.

III. Hippocrates having cured many sicknesses, fell sick himselfe and dyed. The Chaldeans and Astrologians having foretold the deaths of divers, were afterwards themselves surprised by the fates. Alexander and Pompeius, and Caius Cæsar, having destroyed so many townes, and cut off in the field so many thousands both of horse and foot, yet they themselves at last, were faine to part with their owne lives. Heraclitus having written so many naturall tracts concerning the last and generall conflagration of the world, dyed afterwards all filled with water within, and all bedawbed with durt and dung without. Lyce killed Democritus; and Socrates, another sort of vermine, wicked ungodly men. How then stands the case? Thou hast taken

ship, thou hast sailed, thou art come to land, goe **Keep thy**
out, if to another life, there also shalt thou finde **thoughts**
gods, who are every where. If all life and sense
shall cease, then shalt thou cease also to be subject to either paines, or pleasures; and to serve
and tend this vile cottage; so much the viler, by
how much that which ministers unto it doth
excell; the one being a rationall substance, and
a spirit, the other nothing but earth and blood.

IV. Spend not the remnant of thy dayes in
thoughts and phancies concerning other men,
when it is not in relation to some common good,
when by it thou art hindred from some other
better worke. That is, spend not thy time in
thinking, what such a man doth, and to what
end: what he saith, and what he thinkes, and
what he is about, and such other things or curiosities, which make a man to roave and wander
from the care and observation of that part of
himselfe, which is rationall, and over-ruling.
See therefore in the whole series and connexion
of thy thoughts, that thou be carefull to prevent
whatsoever is idle and impertinent: but especially, whatsoever is curious and malitious: and
thou must use thyselfe to think only of such
things, of which if a man upon a suddaine should
ask thee, what it is that thou art now thinking,
thou mayest answere This, and That; freely and
boldly, that so by thy thoughts it may presently
appear that all in thee is sincere, and peaceable;
as becommeth one that is made for society, and
regards not pleasures, nor gives way to any voluptuous imaginations at all: free from all con-

Unspotted by pleasure, undaunted by pain

tentiousnesse, envie, and suspition, and **from** whatsoever else thou wouldest blush to confesse, thy thoughts were set upon. He that is such, is hee surely that doth not put off to lay hold on that which is best indeed, a very Priest and Minister of the gods, well acquainted and in good correspondence with Him especially that is seated and placed within himselfe, as in a Temple and sacrarie: To whom also he keepes and preserves himselfe unspotted by pleasure, undaunted by paine; free from any manner of wrong, or contumelie, by himselfe offered unto himselfe: not capable of any evill from others: a wrastler of the best sort, and for the highest prize, that he may not be cast downe by any passion, or affection of his owne; deeply dyed and drenched in righteousnesse, embracing and accepting with his whole heart, whatsoever either hapneth or is allotted unto him. One who not often, nor without some great necessity tending **to** some publick good, mindeth what any other, either speaks, or doth, or purposeth: for those things onely that are in his owne power, or that are truly his owne, are the objects of his employments, and his thoughts are ever taken up with those things, which of the whole Universe are by the Fates, or Providence destinated and appropriated unto Himselfe. Those things that are his owne, and in his owne power, he himselfe takes order **for** that they be good: and as for those that happen unto him, he beleeves them to bee so. For that lot and portion which is assigned to every one, as it is unavoidable and necessary, so is it alwayes profitable. He remembers besides that whatsoever partakes of reason, is a kinne unto him, and that to care for all men generally, is agreeing to the nature of a man: But as for honour and praise, that they ought not generally to be admitted and accepted of from all, but from such only, who live according to nature. As for them that doe not, what manner of men they be at home, or abroad ; day or night, how conditioned themselves with what manner of conditions, or with men of what conditions they moile and passe away the time together, he knoweth, and remembers right well, he therefore regards not such praise and approbation, as proceeding from them, who cannot like and approve themselves.

Like a soldier waiting for the trumpet

V. Doe nothing against thy will, nor contrary to the communitie, nor without due examination, nor with reluctancie. Affect not to set out thy thoughts with curious neate language. Be neither a great talker, nor a great undertaker. Moreover, let thy god that is in thee to rule over thee, finde by thee, that he hath to doe with a man ; an aged man ; a sociable man ; a Romane ; a Prince; one that hath ordered his life, as one that expecteth, as it were, nothing but the sound of the trumpet, sounding a retreat to depart out of this life with all expedition. One who for his word or actions neither needs an oath, nor any man to be a witnesse.

VI. To be chearefull, and to stand in no need, either of other mens helpe or attendance, or of that rest and tranquillitie, which thou must bee

Follow the best things beholding to others for. Rather like one that is straight of himselfe, or hath ever beene straight, then one that hath beene rectified.

VII. If thou shalt finde any thing in this mortall life better then righteousnesse, then truth, temperance, fortitude, and in generall better then a minde contented both with those things which according to right and reason shee doth, and in those, which without her will and knowledge happen unto thee by the Providence ; If I say, thou canst finde out any thing better then this ; apply thy selfe unto it with thy whole heart, and that which is best wheresoever thou dost finde it, injoy freely. But if nothing thou shalt finde worthy to be preferred to that Spirit which is within thee ; if nothing better then to subject unto thee thine owne lusts and desires, and not to give way to any fancies or imaginations before thou hast duely considered of them, nothing better then to withdraw thy selfe (to use Socrates his words) from all sensualitie, and submit thy selfe unto the gods, and to have care of all men in generall : If thou shalt finde that all other things in comparison of this, are but vile, and of little moment ; then give not way to any other thing, which being once though but affected and inclined unto, it will no more be in thy power, without all distraction as thou oughtest to preferre and to pursue after that good, which is thine owne and thy proper good. For it is not lawfull, that any thing that is of another and inferiour kind and nature, be it what it will, as either popular applause, or honour, or riches, or pleasures; should be suffered to confront and **Prefer** contest as it were, with that which is rationall, **the** and operatively good. For all these things, if **rational** once though but for a while, they beginne to **part** please, **they** presently prevaile, and pervert a mans mind, or turne a man from the right way. Doe thou therefore I say absolutely and freely make choise of that which is best, and stick unto it. Now, that they say is best, which is most profitable. If they meane profitable to man as he is a rationall man, stand thou to it, and maintaine it; but if they meane profitable, as he is a creature, only reject it; and from this thy Tenet, and Conclusion keepe off carefully, all plausible shewes, and colours of externall appearance, that thou maist be able to discerne things rightly.

VIII. Never esteeme of any thing as profitable, which shall ever constraine thee either to breake thy faith, or to lose thy modestie; to hate any man, to suspect, to curse, to dissemble, to lust after any thing, that requireth the secret of walls, or vailes. But he that preferreth before all things his Rationall part and Spirit, and the sacred mysteries of vertue which issueth from it, he shall **never** lament and exclame; never sigh, he shall never want either solitude or company: and which is chiefest of all, he shall live without either desire or feare. And **as** for life, whether for a long or short time **he** shall enjoy his soule thus compassed about with a body, he is altogether indifferent. For if even now he were to depart, he is as ready for it, as for any other action, which may be performed with modestie, and decencie. For all his life long, this is his onely care, that his minde may alwayes be occupied in such intentions and objects, as are proper to a rationall sociable creature.

<small>The disciplined mind</small>

IX. In the minde that is once truly disciplined and purged, thou canst not finde any thing, either foule or impure, or as it were festered: nothing that is either servile, or affected: no partiall tie; no malicious aversenesse; nothing obnoxious; nothing concealed. The life of such an one, Death can never surprise as imperfect; as of an Actour, that should dye before he had ended, or the play it selfe were at an end, a man might speake.

X. Use thine opinative facultie with all honour and respect, for in her indeed is all: that thy opinion doe not beget in thy understanding any thing contrary to either Nature, or the proper constitution of a Rationall creature. The end and object of a Rationall constitution, is, to doe nothing rashly, to bee kindly affected towards men, and in all things willingly to submit unto the gods. Casting therefore all other things aside, keepe thy selfe to these few, and remember withall that no man properly, can be said to live more then that which is now present, which is but a moment of time. Whatsoever is besides either is already past, or incertaine. The time therefore that any man doth live, is but a little, and the place where he liveth, is but a very little corner of the earth, and the greatest fame that can remaine of a man after his Death, even that is but little, and that too, such as it is whilest it **Under-** is, is by the succession of silly mortall men pre- **stand** served, who likewise shall shortly die, and even **things as** whiles they live know not what in very deed they **they are** themselves are : and much lesse can know one, who long before is dead and gone.

XI. To these ever present helpes and mementoes, let one more be added, Ever to make a particular description and delineation as it were of every object that presents it selfe to thy minde, that thou maist wholly and throughly contemplate it, in its owne proper nature, bare and naked ; wholly, and severally ; divided into its severall parts and quarters: and then by thy selfe in thy minde, to call both it, and those things of which it doth consist, and in which it shall be resolved, by their owne proper true Names, and appellations. For there is nothing so effectuall to beget true Magnanimitie, as to be able truly and methodically to examine and consider all things that happen in this life, and so to penetrate into their natures, that at the same time, this also may concurre in our apprehensions : What is the true use of it? and what is the true nature of this Universe, to which it is usefull? How much in regard of the Universe may it bee esteemed? how much in regard of man, a Citizen of the supreame Citie, of which all other Cities in the World, are as it were but houses and families?

XII. What is this, that now my fancy is set upon? of what things doth it consist? how long can it last? which of all the vertues, is the

Preserve thy spirit pure proper vertue for this present use? as whether meeknesse, fortitude, truth, faith, sinceritie, contentation, or any of the rest? Of every thing therefore thou must use thy selfe to say, This immediately comes from God, This by that fatall connexion and concatenation of things, or (which almost comes to one) by some coincidentall casualty. And as for this, it proceeds from my neighbour, my kinsman, my fellow: through his ignorance indeed, because he knowes not what is truly naturall unto him: But I know it, and therefore carry my selfe towards him according to the naturall law of fellowship; that is kindly, and justly. As for those things that of themselves are altogether indifferent, as in my best judgement I conceive every thing to deserve more or lesse, so I carry my selfe towards it.

XIII. If thou shalt intend that which is present, following the rule of right and reason carefully, solidly, meekly, and shalt not intermixe any other businesses, but shalt studie this onely to preserve thy Spirit impolluted, and pure, and shalt cleave unto Him without either hope or feare of any thing, in all things that thou shalt either doe or speake, contenting thy selfe with Heroicall truth, thou shalt live happily; and from this, there is no man that can hinder thee.

XIV. As Physitians and Chirurgions have alwayes their instruments ready at hand for all suddaine cures; so have thou alwayes thy Dogmata in a readinesse for the knowledge of things, both divine and humane: and whatsoever thou dost, even in the smallest things that thou dost, thou must ever remember that mutuall relation, and connexion that is between these two things divine, and things humane. For without relation unto God, thou shalt never speed in any worldly actions; nor on the other side in any divine, without some respect had to things humane.

Body, Soul, and Understanding

XV. Bee not deceived; For thou shalt never live to read thy morall Commentaries, nor the Acts of the famous Romanes and Grecians; nor those Excerpta from severall Bookes; all which thou hadst provided and laid up for thy selfe, against thine old age. Hasten therefore to an end, and giving over all vaine hopes, helpe thy selfe in time if thou carest for thy selfe, as thou oughtest to doe.

XVI. To steale, to sow, to buy, to be at rest, to see what is to be done (which is not seene by the eyes, but by another kinde of sight:) what these words meane, and how many wayes to bee understood, they doe not understand. The Body, the Soule, the Understanding. As the senses naturally, belong to the body, and the desires and affections to the soule, so doe the dogmata to the understanding.

XVII. To be capable of fancies and imaginations, is common to man and beast. To be violently drawne and moved by the lusts and desires of the soule, is proper to wilde beasts and monsters; such as Phalaris, and Nero were. To follow reason for ordinary duties and actions, is common to them also, who beleeve not that there be any gods, and for their advantage would

The true property of a good man   make no conscience to betray their owne Countrey; and who when once the doores be shut upon them, dare doe any thing. If therefore all things else be common to these likewise, it followes, that for a man to like and embrace all things that happen and are destinated unto him, and not to trouble and molest that Spirit which is seated in the temple of his owne breast, with a multitude of vaine fancies, and imaginations, but to keepe him propitious and to obey him as a god, never either speaking any thing contrary to truth, or doing any thing contrary to Justice; is the only true property of a good man. And such a one, though no man should beleeve that he liveth as he doth, either sincerely and conscionably; or cheerefull and contentedly; yet is he neither with any man at all angry for it, nor diverted by it from the way that leadeth to the end of his life, through which a man must passe pure, ever ready to depart, and willing of himselfe without any compulsion to fit and accommodate himselfe to his proper lot and portion.

The Fourth Booke

THAT inward mistris part of man if it be in its owne true naturall temper, is towards all worldly chances and events ever so disposed and affected, that it will easily turne and apply it selfe to that which may bee, and is within its owne power to compasse, when that cannot bee

which at first it intended. For it never doth **Retire**
absolutely addict and apply it selfe to any one **within**
object, but whatsoever it is that it doth now **thyself**
intend and prosecute, it doth prosecute it with
exception and reservation; so that whatsoever
it is that falls out contrary to its first intentions,
even that afterwards it makes its proper object.
Even as the fire when it prevailes upon those
things that are in his way; by which things
indeed a little fire would have beene quenched,
but a great fire doth soone turne to its owne
nature, and so consume whatsoever comes in his
way : yea by those very things it is made greater
and greater.

II. Let nothing be done rashly, and at ran-
dome, but all things according to the most exact
and perfect rules of art.

III. They seeke for themselves private retiring
places, as countrey villages, the sea shoare, moun-
tains; yea thou thy selfe art wont to long much
after such places. But all this thou must know proceeds from simplicitie in the highest degree. At
what time soever thou wilt, it is in thy power, to
retire into thy selfe, and to bee at rest, and free
from all businesses. A man cannot any whither
retire better, then to his owne soule. He especially
who is before hand provided of such things within,
which whensoever hee doth withdraw himselfe
to looke in, may presently afford unto him perfect
ease and tranquillity. By tranquillity I understand a decent orderly disposition and carriage,
free from all confusion and tumultuousnesse.
Afford then thy selfe this retiring continually,

What should offend thee? and thereby refresh and renew thy selfe. Let these precepts be briefe and fundamentall, which as soon as thou doest call them to minde, **may** suffice thee to purge thy soule throughly, and to send thee away well pleased with those things whatsoever they bee, which now againe after this short withdrawing of thy soule into her selfe thou doest returne unto. For what is it that thou art offended at? Can it be at the wickednesse of men, when thou doest call to minde this conclusion, that all reasonable creatures are made one for another? and that it is part of justice to beare with them? and that it is against their wills that they offend? and how many already, who once likewise prosecuted their enmities, suspected, hated, and fiercely contended, are now long agoe stretcht out, and reduced unto Ashes? It is time for thee to make an end. As for those things which among the common chances of the world happen unto thee as thy particular lot and portion, canst thou be displeased with any of them, when thou doest call that our ordinary Dilemma to minde, Either a Providence, or Democritus his Atomes; and with it, whatsoever we brought to prove, that the whole world is as it were one Citie? And as for thy body, what canst thou feare, if thou doest consider that thy Minde and Understanding, when once it hath recollected it selfe, and knowes its owne power, hath in this life and Breath, (whether it runne smoothly and gently, or whether harshly and rudely,) no interest at all, but is altogether indifferent: and whatsoever else thou hast heard and assented unto concerning either paine or pleasure? But the care of thine honour and reputation will perchance distract thee? How can that be, if thou doest look back, and consider both how quickly all things that are, are forgotten, and what an immense chaos of eternity was before, and will follow after all things: and the vanity of praise, and the inconstancie and variablenesse of humane Judgements and opinions, and the narrownesse of the place, wherein it is limited and circumscribed? For the whole earth is but as one point; and of it, this inhabited part of it, is but a very little part; and of this part, how many in number, and what manner of men are they, that will commend thee? What remaines then, but that thou often put in practise this kinde of retyring of thy selfe, to this little part of thy selfe; and above all things, keepe thy selfe from distraction, and intend not any thing vehemently, but be free and consider all things, as a man, whose proper object is vertue, as a man whose true nature is to be kinde and sociable, as a Citizen, as a mortall creature. Among other things, which to consider, and looke into thou must use to withdraw thy selfe, let those two be among the most obvious and at hand. One, that the things or objects themselves, reach not unto the soule, but stand without still, and quiet, and that it is from the opinion only which is within, that all the tumult and all the trouble doth proceed. The next, that all these things, which now thou seest, shall within a very little while be changed, and bee no more: and ever call to minde, how many

Keep thyself from distraction

The world is as it were one City

changes and alterations in the world thou thy selfe hast already been an eye witnesse of in thy time. This world is meere change, and this life, opinion.

IV. If to understand and to be reasonable be common unto all men, then is that reason, for which we **are** termed reasonable, common unto all. If reason in generall, then is that reason also, which prescribeth what is to be done and what not, common unto all. If that, then Law. If Law, then are we fellow Citizens. If so, then are we partners in some one common weale. If so, then the world is as it were a Citie. **For** which other common weale is it, that all men can be said to be members of? From this common Citie it is, that Understanding, Reason, and Law is derived unto us, for from whence **else**? For as that which in me is earthly I have from some common earth; and that which is moist from some other Element is imparted; as my breath and life hath its proper fountaine; and that likewise which is dry and fiery in me: (for there is nothing which doth not proceed from something; as also there is nothing that can be reduced unto meere nothing:) so also is there some common beginning from whence my understanding hath proceeded.

V. As generation is, so also death, a secret of Natures Wisedome: a mixture of Elements, resolved into the same Elements againe, a thing surely which no man ought to be ashamed of: in a series of other fatall events and consequences, which a rationall creature is subject unto, not improper or incongruous, nor contrary to the naturall and proper constitution of man himselfe.

All things happen justly

VI. Such and such things, from such and such causes, must of necessity proceed. Hee that would not have such things to happen, is as he that would have the fig-tree grow without any sappe or moisture. In summe, remember this, that within a very little while, both thou and he shall both be dead, and after a little while more, not so much as your names and memories shall be remaining.

VII. Let opinion be taken away, and no man will thinke himselfe wronged. If no man shall think himselfe wronged, then is there no more any such thing as wrong. That which makes not man himselfe the worse, cannot make his life the worse, neither can it hurt him either inwardly or outwardly. It was expedient in nature that it should be so, and therefore necessary.

VIII. Whatsoever doth happen in the world, doth happen justly, and so if thou dost well take heed, thou shalt finde it. I say not only in right order by a series of inevitable consequences, but according to Justice and as it were by way of equall distribution, according to the true worth of every thing. Continue then to take notice of it, as thou hast begunne, and whatsoever thou doest, doe it not without this proviso, that it be a thing of that nature that a good man, (as the word good is properly taken) may doe it. This observe carefully in every action.

IX. Conceit no such things, as he that wrongeth thee conceiveth, or would have thee to conceive, but looke into the matter it selfe, and see what it is in very truth.

<small>Act for the benefit of mankind</small>

X. These two rules, thou must have alwayes in a readinesse. First doe nothing at all, but what Reason proceeding from that Regall and supreme part, shall for the good and benefit of men, suggest unto thee. And secondly, if any man that is present, shall be able to rectifie thee or to turne thee from some erroneous perswasion, that thou be alwayes ready to change thy minde, and this change to proceed, not from any respect of any pleasure or credit thereon depending, but alwayes from some probable appearant ground of Justice, or of some publick good thereby to be farthered; or from some other such inducement.

XI. Hast thou reason? I have. Why then makest thou not use of it? For if thy reason doe her part, what more canst thou require?

XII. As a part hitherto thou hast had a particular subsistence: and now shalt thou vanish away into the common substance of Him, who first begot thee, or rather thou shalt be resumed againe into that original rational substance, out of which all others have issued, and are propagated. Many small peeces of frankincense are set upon the same altar, one drops first and is consumed, another after; and it comes all to one.

XIII. Within tenne dayes, if so happen, thou shalt be esteemed a god of them, who now if **thou** shalt returne to the Dogmata and to the honouring of Reason, will esteeme of thee no better then of a meere brute, and of an ape.

XIV. Not as though thou hadst thousands of yeares to live. Death hangs over thee: whilest yet thou livest, whilest thou maiest, be good.

What is Fame?

XV. How much time and leisure doth he gaine, who is not curious to know, what his neighbour hath said, or hath done, or hath attempted, but only what he doth himselfe, that it may be just and holy? or to expresse it in Agathos words, Not to looke about upon the evill conditions of others, but to runne on straight in the line, without any loose, and extravagant agitation.

XVI. Hee who is greedy of credit and reputation after his death, doth not consider, that they themselves by whom he is remembred, shall soone after every one of them be dead; And they likewise **that succeed** those; untill at last all memorie, which hitherto by the succession of men admiring and soone after dying hath had its course, be quite extinct. But suppose that both they that shall remember thee, and thy memory with them should be immortall, what is that to thee? I will not say to thee after thou art dead; but even to thee living, what is thy praise? But only for a secret and politick consideration, which **wee** call οἰκονομίαν, or Dispensation. For as for that, that it is the gift of nature, whatsoever is commended in thee, what might be objected from thence, let that now that wee are upon another consideration, be omitted as unseasonable. That which is faire and goodly, whatsoever it be, and in what respect soever it be, that it is faire and goodly, it is so of it selfe, and terminates in it selfe, not admitting praise as a part or member:

Does the soul continue after death? that therefore which is praised, is not thereby made either better or worse. This I understand even of those things, that are commonly called faire and good, as those which are commended either for the matter it selfe, or for curious workmanship. As for that which is truly good, what can it stand in need of more, then either Justice or Truth; or more then either kindnesse and modestie? Which of all those, either becomes good or faire, because commended; or dispraised suffers any dammage? Doth the Emrald become worse in it selfe, or more vile if it be not commended? Doth gold, or yvory, or purple? Is there anything that doth though never so common, as a knife, a flower or a tree?

XVII. If so be that the soules remaine after death (say they that will not beleeve it); how is the aire from all eternitie able to containe them? How is the earth (say I) ever from that time able to containe the bodyes of them that are buried? For as here the change and resolution of dead bodyes into another kinde of subsistence, (whatsoever it be;) makes place for other dead bodies: so the soules after death transferred into the aire, after they have conversed there a while, are either by way of transmutation, or transfusion, or conflagration, received againe into that originall rationall substance, from which all others doe proceed: and so give way to those soules, who before coupled and associated unto bodyes, now beginne to subsist single. This, upon a supposition that the soules after death doe for a while subsist single, may be answered. And here, (besides *O Nature,* the number of bodies, so buried and contained by *from thee* the earth), we may further consider the number *are all* of severall beasts, eaten by us men, and by other *things* creatures. For notwithstanding that such a multitude of them is daily consumed, and as it were buried in the bodyes of the eaters, yet is the same place and body able to containe them, by reason of their conversion, partly into blood, partly into aire and fire. What in these things is the speculation of truth? to divide things into that which is passive, and materiall; and that which is active and formall.

XVIII. Not to wander out of the way, but upon every motion and desire, to perform that which is just: and ever to be carefull to attaine to the true naturall apprehension of every fancie, that presents it selfe.

XIX. Whatsoever is expedient unto thee, O World, is expedient unto me, nothing can either be unseasonable unto me, or out of date, which unto thee is seasonable. Whatsoever thy seasons beare, shall ever by me bee esteemed as happy fruit, and increase. O Nature! from thee are all things, in thee all things subsist, and to thee all tend. Could he say of Athens, Thou lovely Citie of Cecrops; and shalt not thou say of the World, Thou lovely Citie of God?

XX. They will say commonly, Meddle not with many things, if thou wilt live chearefully. Certainely there is nothing better, then for a man to confine himselfe to necessary actions; to such and so many only, as reason in a creature

Avoid unnecessary actions and thoughts. that knowes it selfe borne for society, will command and enjoyne. This will not onely procure that chearfulnesse, which from the goodnesse, but that also, which from the paucitie of actions doth usually proceed. For since it is so, that most of those things, which wee either speake or doe, are unnecessary; if a man shall cut them off, it must needs follow that he shall thereby gaine much leisure, and save much trouble, and therefore at every action a man must privately by way of admonition suggest unto himselfe, What? may not this that now I goe about, be of the number of unnecessary actions? Neither must he use himselfe to cut off actions only, but thoughts and imaginations also, that are unnecessary; for so will unnecessary consequent actions the better be prevented and cut off.

XXI. Trie also how a good mans life; (of one, who is well pleased with those things whatsoever, which among the common changes and chances of this world fall to his owne lot and share; and can live well contented and fully satisfied in the justice of his owne proper present action, and in the goodnesse of his disposition for the future:) will agree with thee. Thou hast had experience of that other kinde of life: make now tryall of this also. Trouble not thy selfe any more henceforth, reduce thy selfe unto perfect simplicity. Doth any man offend? It is against himselfe that he doth offend: why should it trouble thee? Hath any thing happened unto thee? It is well, whatsoever it be, it is that which of all the common chances of the world Life is from the very beginning in the series of all other short things that have, or shall happen, was destinated and appointed unto thee. To comprehend all in few words; Our life is short; wee must endeavour to gaine the present time with best discretion and justice. Use recreation with sobriety.

XXII. Either this world is a Κόσμος, or a comely peece, because all disposed and governed by certaine order: or if it be a mixture, though confused, yet still it is a Κόσμος, a comely peece. For is it possible that in thee there should be any beauty at all, and that in the whole world there should be nothing but disorder, and confusion? and all things in it too, by natural different properties one from another differenced, and distinguished; and yet all through diffused, and by naturall Sympathie, one to another united, as they are?

XXIII. A black, or maligne disposition, an effeminate disposition; an hard inexorable disposition, a wilde inhumane disposition, a sheepish disposition, a childish disposition; a blockish, a false, a scurril, a fraudulent, a tyrannicall: what then? If he be a stranger in the world, that knowes not the things that are in it; why not he a stranger as well, that wonders at the things that are done in it?

XXIV. He is a true fugitive, that flyes from reason, by which men are sociable. Hee blinde, who cannot see with the eyes of his understanding. He poore, that stands in need of another,

Trust in the Gods — and hath not in himselfe all things needfull for this life. Hee an Aposteme of the world, who by being discontented with those things that happen unto him in the world, doth as it were Apostatize, and separate himselfe from Common Natures rationall Administration. For the same nature it is that brings this unto thee, whatsoever it be, that first brought thee into the world. He raises sedition in the Citie, who by irrationall actions withdrawes his owne soule from that One and common soule of all rationall Creatures.

XXV. There is, who without so much as a Coat; and there is, who without so much as a booke, doth put philosophie in practice. I am halfe naked, neither have I bread to eate, and yet I depart not from Reason, saith one. But I say; I want the food of good teaching, and instructions, and yet I depart not from Reason.

XXVI. What art, and profession soever thou hast learned, endeavour to affect it, and comfort thy selfe in it; and passe the remainder of thy life as one who from his whole heart commits himselfe and whatsoever belongs unto him, unto the gods, and as for men, carry not thy selfe either tyrannically or servilely towards any.

XXVII. Consider in thy minde, for examples sake, the times of Vespasian: Thou shalt see but the same things: some marying, some bringing up children, some sick, some dying, some fighting, some feasting, some merchandizing, some tilling, some flattering, some boasting, some suspecting, some undermining, some wishing to die, some fretting and murmuring at their present estate,

some wooing, some hoarding, some seeking after **Be not**
Magistracies, and some after Kingdomes. And **anxious**
is not that their age quite over, and ended? **over**
Againe, consider now the times of Trajan. **trifles**
There likewise thou seest the very selfe-same
things, and that age also is now over and ended.
In the like manner consider other periods, both
of times, and of whole nations, and see how
many men, after they had with all their might
and main intended, and prosecuted some one
worldly thing or other, did soone after drop
away, and were resolved into the Elements.
But especially thou must call to minde them,
whom thou thy selfe in thy life time hast knowne
much distracted about vaine things, and in the
meane time neglecting to doe that, and closely,
and unseparably (as fully satisfied with it) to
adhere unto it, which their owne proper constitution
did require. And here thou must remember,
that thy carriage in every businesse must be
according to the worth, and due proportion of it,
for so shalt thou not easily be tyred out and
vexed, if thou shalt not dwel upon small matters
longer then is fitting.

XXVIII. Those words which once were
common and ordinary, are now become obscure,
and obsolet; and so the names of men once
commonly knowne and famous, are now become
in a manner obscure, and obsolet names.
Camillus, Cæso, Volesius, Leonnatus; not long
after, Scipio, Cato, then Augustus, then Adrianus,
then Antoninus Pius: All these in a short
time will be out of date, and, as things of an-

All is vanity other world as it were, become fabulous. And this I say of them, who once shined as the wonders of their ages, for as for the rest, no sooner are they expired, then with them all their fame and memorie. And what is it then that shall alwayes be remembred? all is vanity. What is it that wee must bestow our care and diligence upon? even upon this only: That our minds and wils be just; that our actions be charitable; that our speech be never deceitfull, or that our understanding bee not subject to error; that our inclination be alwayes set to embrace whatsoever shall happen unto us, as necessary, as usuall, as ordinary, as flowing from such a beginning, and such a fountaine, from which both thou thy selfe, and all things are. Willingly therefore, and wholly surrender up thy selfe unto that fatall concatenation, yeelding up thy selfe unto the fates, to be disposed of at their pleasure.

XXIX. Whatsoever is now present, and from day to day hath its existence; all objects of memories, and the mindes and memories themselves, incessantly consider, all things that are, have their being by change, and alteration. Use thy selfe therefore often to meditate upon this, that the Nature of the Universe delights in nothing more, then in altering those things that are, and in making others like unto them. So that wee may say, that whatsoever is, is but as it were the seed of that which shall be. For if thou thinke that that only is seed, which either the Earth, or the wombe receiveth, thou art very simple.

XXX. Thou art now ready to dye, and yet hast thou not attained to that perfect simplicity: thou art yet subject to many troubles, and perturbations; not yet free from all feare and suspition of externall accidents; nor yet either so meekly disposed towards all men, as thou shouldest; or so affected as one, whose only study, and only wisedome is, to be just in all his actions. *Thy body is but the cottage of thy soul*

XXXI. Behold and observe, what is the state of their rationall part; and those that the world doth account wise, see what things they flie, and are afraid of; and what things they hunt after.

XXXII. In another mans minde and understanding thy evill cannot subsist, nor in any proper temper or distemper of the naturall constitution of thy body, which is but as it were the coate, or cottage of thy soule. Wherein then, but in that part of thee, wherein the conceit, and apprehension of any misery can subsist? Let not that part therefore admit any such conceit, and then all is well. Though thy body which is so neere it, should either be cut or burnt, or suffer any corruption, or putrefaction, yet let that part to which it belongs to judge of these, be still at rest; that is, Let her judge this, that, whatsoever it is, that equally may happen to a wicked man, and to a good man, is neither good, nor evill. For that which happens equally to him that lives according to Nature, and to him that doth not, is neither according to nature, nor against it; and by consequent, neither good, nor bad.

Time like an ever rolling stream

XXXIII. Ever consider and thinke upon the world, as being but one living substance, and having but one soule, and how all things in the world, are terminated, into one sensitive power; and are done by one generall motion as it were, and deliberation of that one soule; and how all things that are, concurre in the cause of one anothers being, and by what **manner** of connexion and concatenation all things happen.

XXXIV. What art thou, that better and divine part excepted, but as Epictetus said well, a wretched soule, appointed to carry a carcasse up and downe?

XXXV. To suffer change, can be no hurt; as no benefit it is, by change to attaine to being. The age and time of the world is as it were a flood, and swift current, consisting of the things that are brought to passe in the world. For as soone as any thing hath appeared, and is passed away, another succeeds, and that also will presently out of sight.

XXXVI. Whatsoever doth happen in the world, is, in the course of nature, as usuall and ordinarie as a rose in the spring, and fruit in summer. Of the same nature is sicknesse and death; slaunder, and lying in waite, and whatsoever else ordinarily doth unto fooles use to be occasion either of joy or sorrow. That, whatsoever it is, that comes after, doth alwayes very naturally, and as it were familiarly, follow upon that which was before. For thou must consider the things of the world, **not as** a loose independent number, consisting meerely of necessary **Death of** events; but as a discreet connexion of things **the ele-** orderly and harmoniously disposed. There is **ments** then to be seen in the things of the world, not a bare succession, but an admirable correspondence and affinitie.

XXXVII. Let that of Heraclitus never be out of thy minde, that the death of earth, is water, and the death of water, is aire; and the death of aire, is fire; and so on the contrary. Remember him also who was ignorant whither the way did lead, and how that Reason being the thing, by which all things in the world are administred, and which men are continually and most inwardly conversant with: yet is the thing, which ordinarily they are most in opposition with, and how those things which daily happen among them, cease not daily to be strange unto them, and that we should not either speake, or doe anything as men in their sleepe, by opinion and bare imagination: for then wee thinke wee speake and doe, and that we must not be as children, who follow their fathers example; for best reason alleaging their bare καθότι παρειλήφαμεν; or, As by successive tradition from our forefathers wee have received it.

XXXVIII. Even as if any of the gods should tell thee, thou shalt certainely die to morrow, or next day, thou wouldest not, except thou wert extreamly base, and pusillanimous, take it for a great benefit, rather to dy the next day after, then to morrow; (for alas what is the difference!) so, for the same reason,

What is man? thinke it no great matter to die rather many yeares after, then the very next day.

XXXIX. Let it be thy perpetuall meditation, how many physitians who once looked so grimme, and so tetrically shrunk their browes upon their patients, are dead and gone themselves. How many Astrologers, after that in great ostentation they had foretold the death of some others, how many Philosophers after so many elaborate tracts and volumes concerning either mortality, or immortality; how many brave Captaines and Commanders, after the death and slaughter of so many: how many Kings and Tyrants, after they had with such horror and insolencie abused their power upon mens lives, as though themselves had beene immortall; how many, that I may so speake, whole Cities both men and Townes: Helice, Pompeii, Herculaneum, and others innumerable are dead and gone. Runne them over also, whom thou thyselfe, one after another, hast known in thy time to drop away. Such and such a one tooke care of such and such a ones burial, and soone after was buried himselfe. So one, so another: and all things in a short time. For herein lyeth all indeed, ever to looke upon all worldly things, as things for their continuance, that last but from day to day; or, that are but for a day: and for their worth, most vile, and contemptible, as for example, What is man? That which but the other day when hee was conceived was vile snivell; and within few dayes shall be eyther an embalmed carkasse, or mere ashes. Thus must

thou according to truth and nature, throughly *Storm-*
consider, how mans life is but for a very moment *beaten,*
of time, and so depart meeke, and contented : *but un-*
even as if a ripe Olive falling, should praise the *moved*
ground that bare her, and give thankes to the
tree that begat her.

XL. Thou must be like a promontarie of the sea, against which though the waves beare continually, yet it both it selfe stands, and about it are those swelling waves stilled and quieted.

XLI. Oh, wretched I! to whom this mischance is happened! nay, happy I, to whom this thing being happened, I can continue without griefe; neither wounded by that which is present, nor in feare of that which is to come. For as for this, it might have happened unto any man, but any man having such a thing befallen him, could not have continued without griefe. Why then should that rather be an unhappinesse, then this a happinesse? But however, canst thou, O man! terme that unhappinesse, which is no mischance to the nature of man! Canst thou thinke that a mischance to the nature of man, which is not contrary to the end and will of his nature? What then hast thou learned is the will of mans nature? Doth that then which hath happened unto thee, hinder thee from being just? or magnanimous? or temperate? or wise? or circumspect? or true? or modest? or free? or from anything else of all those things in the present enjoying and possession whereof the nature of man, (as then enjoying all that is proper unto her,) is fully satisfied? Now to conclude;

A remedy against the fear of death upon all occasion of sorrow remember henceforth to make use of this Dogma, that whatsoever it is that hath happened unto thee, is in very deed no such thing of it selfe, as a misfortune; but that to beare it generously, is certainely great happinesse.

XLII. It is but an ordinary coorse one, yet it is a good effectuall remedy against the feare of death, for a man to consider in his minde the examples of such, who greedily and covetously (as it were) did for a long time enjoy their lives. What have they got more, then they whose deaths have beene untimely? Are not they themselves dead at the last? as Cadicianus, Fabius, Julianus, Lepidus, or any other who in their life time having buried many, were at the last buried themselves. The whole space of any mans life, is but little; and as little as it is, with what troubles, with what manner of dispositions, and in the society of how wretched a body must it be passed! Let it be therefore unto thee altogether as a matter of indifferencie. For if thou shalt looke backward; behold, what an infinite Chaos of time doth present it selfe unto thee; and as infinite a Chaos, if thou shalt looke forward. In that which is so infinite, what difference can there bee betweene that which liveth but three dayes, and that which liveth three ages?

XLIII. Let thy course ever be, the most compendious way. The most compendious, is that which is according to nature: that is, in all both words and deeds, ever to follow that which is most sound and perfect. For such a resolution will free a man from all trouble, strife, dissembling, and ostentation.

Whereto wert thou born?

The Fifth Booke

IN the morning when thou findest thyselfe unwilling to rise, consider with thyselfe presently, it is to goe about a mans worke that I am stirred up. Am I then yet unwilling to goe about that, for which I myselfe was borne and brought forth into this world? Or was I made for this, to lay me downe, and make much of myself in a warme bed? O but this is pleasing. And was it then for this that thou wert borne, that thou mightest enjoy pleasure? Was it not in very truth for this, that thou mightest alwayes be busie and in action? Seest thou not how all things in the world besides, how every tree and plant, how sparrowes and ants, spiders and bees: how all in their kinde are intent as it were orderly to performe whatsoever (towards the preservation of this orderly Universe) naturally doth become and belong unto them? And wilt not thou doe that, which belongs unto a man to doe? Wilt not thou runne to doe that, which thy nature doth require? But thou must have some rest. Yes, thou must. Nature hath of that also, as well as of eating and drinking, allowed thee a certaine stint. But thou goest beyond thy stint, and beyond that which would suffice, and in matter

Honour thy nature of action, there thou comest short of that which thou maist. It must needs be therefore, that thou dost not love thyselfe, for if thou didst, thou wouldst also love thy Nature, and that which thy nature doth propose unto herself as **her end.** Others, as many as take pleasure in their trade and profession, can even pine themselves at their workes, and neglect their bodies and their food for it; and doest thou lesse honour thy nature, then an ordinary mechanick his trade; or a good dancer his art? then a covetous man his silver, and a vaine glorious man applause? These to whatsoever they take an affection, can be content to want their meat and sleepe, to further that every one which he affects: and shall actions tending to the common good of humane societie, seeme more vile unto thee, or worthy of lesse respect, and intention?

II. How easie a thing is it for a man to put off from him all turbulent adventitious imaginations, and presently to be in perfect rest and tranquillity?

III. Thinke thyselfe fit and worthy to speake, or to doe any thing, that is according to Nature, and let not the reproach, or report of some that may ensue upon it, ever deterre thee. If it be right and honest to be spoken or done, undervalue not thyselfe so much, as to be discouraged from it. As for them, they have their owne rationall over-ruling part, and their owne proper inclination: which thou must not stand and looke about to take notice of, but goe on straight, whither both thine owne particular, and the common nature doe lead thee; and the way of both these, is but one.

IV. I continue my course by actions according to nature, untill I fall and cease, breathing out my last breath into that aire, by which continually breathed in I did live; and falling upon that earth, out of whose gifts and fruits my father gathered his seed, my mother her blood, and my nurse her milk, out of which for so many yeares I have beene provided, both of meate and drinke. And lastly, which beareth mee that tread upon it, and beareth with me that so many wayes doe abuse it, or so freely make use of it, so many wayes to so many ends.

V. No man can admire thee for thy sharpe acute language, such is thy naturall disabilitie that way. Be it so: yet there be many other good things, for the want of which thou canst not pleade the want of naturall abilitie. Let them be seene in thee, which depend wholly from thee; sincerity, gravity, laboriousnesse, contempt of pleasures; be not querulous, be content with little, be kinde, be free; avoid all superfluitie, all vaine pratling; be magnanimous. Doest not thou perceive, how many things there be, which notwithstanding any pretence of naturall indisposition and unfitnesse, thou mightest have performed and exhibited, and yet still thou doest voluntarily continue drooping downewards? Or wilt thou say, that it is through defect of thy naturall constitution, that thou art constrained to murmur, to be base and wretched; to flatter; now to accuse, and now to please, and pacifie

Plead not want of ability

For a good turn seek no return thy body: to bee vaine-glorious, to bee so guidy headed, and unsetled in thy thoughts? nay (witnesses bee the Gods) of all these thou mightest have beene rid long agoe: Only, this thou must have beene contented with, to have borne the blame of one that is somewhat slow and dull. Wherein thou must so exercise thyselfe, as one who neither doth much take to heart this his naturall defect, nor yet pleaseth himselfe in it.

VI. Such there be, who when they have done a good turne to any, are ready to set them on the score for it, and to require retaliation. Others there be, who though they stand not upon retaliation, to require any, yet they thinke with themselves neverthelesse, that such a one is their debtor, and they know as their word is what they have done. Others againe there be, who when they have done any such thing, doe not so much as know what they have done; but are like unto the vine, which beareth her grapes, and when once shee hath borne her owne proper fruit, is contented and seekes for no further recompence. As a horse after a race, and a hunting dog when hee hath hunted, and a Bee when she hath made her hony, looke not for applause and commendation; so neither doth that man that rightly doth understand his owne nature when he hath done a good turne: but from one doth proceed to doe another, even as the vine after shee hath once borne fruit in her owne proper season, is ready for another time. Thou therefore must be one of them, who what they do, barely do it without any further thought, and are in a maner unsensible

of what they doe. Nay but, will some reply per- **Pray**
chance, this very thing a rationall man is bound **for the**
unto, to understand what it is, that hee doeth. For **general**
it is the property, say they, of one that is natur- **good**
ally sociable, to be sensible, that hee doth operate
sociably: nay, and to desire, that the partie himselfe that is sociably dealt with, should bee sensible
of it too. I answer; That which thou sayest is
true indeed, but the true meaning of that which is
said, thou dost not understand. And therefore art
thou one of those first, whom I mentioned. For
they also are led by a probable appearance of
reason. But if thou dost desire to understand
truely what it is that is said, feare not that thou
shalt therefore give over any sociable action.

VII. The forme of the Athenians prayer did
runne thus; 'O raine, raine good Iupiter, upon
all the grounds and fields that belong to the
Athenians.' Eyther wee should not pray at all,
or thus absolutely and freely; and not every one
for himselfe in particular alone.

VIII. As wee say commonly, The physitian
hath præscribed unto this man, riding; unto
another, cold baths; unto a third, to goe bare
foot: so it is alike to say, The Nature of the
Universe hath præscribed unto this man sicknesse,
or blindnesse, or some losse, or damage or some
such thing. For as there, when wee say of a physitian, that hee hath præscribed any thing, our
meaning is, that hee hath appointed this for that,
as subordinate and conducing to health: so here,
whatsoever doth happen unto any, is ordained
unto him as a thing subordinate unto the

Nature's physick fates, and therefore doe wee say of such things, that they do συμβαίνειν, that is, happen, or, fall together; as of square stones, when either in wals, or pyramides in a certaine position they fit one another, and agree as it were in an harmony, the Masons say, that they doe συμβαίνειν; as if thou shouldest say, fall together: so that in the generall, though the things be divers that make it, yet the consent or harmony it selfe is but one. And as the whole world is made up of all the particular bodies of the world, one perfect and compleat body, of the same nature that particular bodies; so is the Destiny of particular causes and events one generall one, of the same nature that particular causes are. What I now say, even they that are mere Idiots are not ignorant of: for they say commonly τοῦτο ἔφερεν αὐτῷ, that is, This his Destiny hath brought upon him. This therefore is by the Fates properly and particularly brought upon this, as that unto this in particular is by the physitian præscribed. These therefore let us accept of in like manner, as wee doe those that are præscribed unto us by our Physitians. For them also in themselves shall wee finde to containe many harsh things, but wee neverthelesse, in hope of health, and recovery, accept of them. Let the fulfilling and accomplishment of those things which the common nature hath determined, be unto thee as thy health. Accept then, and be pleased with whatsoever doth happen, though otherwise harsh and unpleasing, as tending to that end, to the health and welfare of the Universe, and to Joves happinesse and prosperity. For this whatsoever it be, should not have beene produced, had it not conduced to the good of the Universe. For neither doth any ordinary particular nature bring any thing to passe, that is not to whatsoever is within the sphere of its owne proper administration and government agreeable and subordinate. For these two considerations then thou must be well pleased with any thing that doth happen unto thee. First, because that for **thee** properly it was brought to passe, and unto thee it was præscribed; and that from the very beginning by the series and connexion of the first causes, it hath ever had a reference unto thee. And secondly, because the good successe and perfect welfare, and indeed the very continuance of Him, that is the Administrator of the whole, doth in a manner depend on it. For the whole (because whole, therefore entire and perfect) is maimed, and mutilated, if thou shalt cut off any thing at all, whereby the coherence, and contiguity (as of parts, so) of causes, is maintained and preserved. Of which certaine it is, that thou doest (as much as lyeth in thee) **cut off**, and in some sort violently take somewhat away, as often as thou art displeased with any thing that happeneth. *(marginal: **What happens to thee is prescribed for thee**)*

IX. Bee not discontented, bee not disheartened, bee not out of hope, if often it succeed not so well with thee punctually and precisely to doe all things according to the right dogmata, but being once cast off, returne unto them againe:

Philosophy to be thy ease and comfort and as for those many and more frequent occurrences, either of worldly distractions, or humane infirmities, which as a man thou canst not but in some measure be subject unto, bee not thou discontented with them; but however, love and affect that only which thou dost returne unto: a Philosophers life, and proper occupation after the most exact manner. And when thou dost returne to thy philosophie, returne not unto it as the manner of some is, after play and liberty as it were, to their School Masters and Pedagogues; but as they that have sore eyes to their sponge and egg: or as another to his cataplasme; or as others to their fomentations: so shalt not thou make it a matter of ostentation at all to obey reason; but of ease and comfort. And remember that philosophie requireth nothing of thee, but what thy nature requireth, and wouldest thou thy selfe desire any thing that is not according to nature? for which of these saiest thou; that which is according to Nature or against it, is of it selfe more kind and pleasing? Is it not for that respect especially, that pleasure it selfe is to so many mens hurt and overthrow, most prevalent, because esteemed commonly most kind, and naturall? But consider well whether magnanimitie rather, and true liberty, and true simplicity, and equanimity, and holines; whether these be not most kinde and naturall? And prudencie it selfe, what more kind and amiable then it, when thou shalt truly consider with thy self, what it is through al the proper objects of thy rational intellectuall faculty currently to go on without any fall or stumble? As for the things of the world, their true nature is in a manner so involved with obscuritie, that unto many philosophers, and those no meane ones, they seemed altogether incomprehensible: and the Stoicks themselves, though they judge them not altogether incomprehensible, yet scarce and not without much difficulty, comprehensible, so that all assent of ours is fallible, for who is he that is infallible in his conclusions? From the nature of things, passe now unto their subjects and matter: how temporary, how vile are they! such as may be in the power and possession of some abominable loose liver, of some common strumpet, of some notorious oppressor and extortioner. Passe from thence to the dispositions of them that thou doest ordinarily converse with, how hardly doe wee beare, even with the most loving and amiable! that I may not say, how hard it is for us to beare even with our owne selves. In such obscurity, and impurity of things: in such and so continuall a fluxe both of the substances and time; both of the motions themselves, and things moved; what it is that we can fasten upon; either to honour, and respect especially; or seriously, and studiously to seeke after; I cannot so much as conceive. For indeed they are things contrary.

How vile are material things!

X. Thou must comfort thy selfe in the expectation of thy naturall dissolution, and in the meane time not grieve at the delay; but rest contented in those two things. First, that nothing shall happen unto thee, which is not according to

What things are good

the nature of the Universe. Secondly, that it is in thy power, to doe nothing against thine owne proper god, and inward Spirit. For it is not in any mans power to constraine thee to transgresse against him.

XI. What is the use that now at this present I make of my soule? Thus from time to time and upon all occasions thou must put this question to thy selfe, what is now that part of mine which they call the rationall mistris part, imployed about? Whose soule doe I now properly possesse? a childes? or a youths? a womans? or a tyrants? some brute, or some wilde beasts soule?

XII. What those things are in themselves, which by the greatest part are esteemed good, thou maist gather even from this. For if a man shall heare things mentioned as good, which are really good indeed, such as are prudence, temperance, justice, fortitude; after so much heard and conceived, hee cannot endure to heare of any more, for the word good is properly spoken of them. But as for those which by the vulgar are esteemed good, if he shall heare them mentioned as good, he doth hearken for more. He is well contented to heare, that what is spoken by the Comædian, is but familiarly and popularly spoken, so that even the vulgar apprehend the difference. For why is it else, that this offends not and needs not to be excused, when vertues are stiled good: but that which is spoken in commendation of wealth, pleasure, or honour, wee entertaine it only as merrily and pleasantly spoken? Proceed therefore, and inquire further, whether it may not bee that those things also which being mentioned upon the stage were merrily, and with great applause of the multitude, scoffed at with this jest, that they that possessed them, had not in all the world of their owne, (such was their affluence and plenty) so much as a place where to avoide their excrements. Whether, I say, these ought not also in very deed to be much respected, and esteemed of, as the only things that are truly good.

Reason contented with itself

XIII. All that I consist of, is either forme or matter. No corruption can reduce either of these unto nothing: for neither did I of nothing become a subsistent creature. Every part of mine then, will by mutation be disposed into a certaine part of the whole world, and that in time into another part; and so *in infinitum;* by which kinde of mutation, I also became what I am, and so did they that begot me, and they before them, and so upwards *in infinitum.* For so we may be allowed to speake, though the age and government of the world, be to some certaine periods of time limited, and confined.

XIV. Reason, and rationall power, are faculties which content themselves with themselves, and their owne proper operations. And as for their first inclination and motion, that they take from themselves. But their progresse is right to the end and object, which is in their way, as it were, and lyeth just before them: that is, which is feasible and possible, whether it be that which at the first they proposed to themselves, or no. For which reason also such actions are termed κατορθώσεις, to intimate the directnesse of the way, by which they are atchieved. Nothing

As thy thoughts, so will thy soul be must be thought to belong to a man, which doth not belong unto him as he is a man. These, the event of purposes, are not things required in a man. The nature of man doth not professe any such things. The finall ends and consummations of actions are nothing at all to a mans nature. The end therefore of a man, or that *summum bonum* whereby that end is fulfilled, cannot consist in the consummation of actions purposed and intended. Againe, concerning these outward worldly things, were it so that any of them did properly belong unto man, then would it not belong unto man, to contemne them and to stand in opposition with them. Neither would hee be praise worthy that can live without them; or he good, (if these were good indeed) who of his owne accord doth deprive himselfe of any of them. But we see contrarywise, that the more a man doth withdraw himselfe from these wherein externall pompe and greatnesse doth consist, or any other like these; or the better he doth beare with the losse of these, the better he is accounted.

XV. Such as thy thoughts and ordinary cogitations are, such will thy minde be in time. For the soule doth as it were receive its tincture from the phancies, and imaginations. Dye it therefore and throughly soke it with the assiduitie of these cogitations. As for example. Wheresoever thou mayest live, there it is in thy power to live well and happy. But thou mayest live at the Court, there then also mayest thou live well and happy. Againe, that which every thing is made for, he is also made unto that, and cannot but naturally incline unto it. That which **Society** any thing doth naturally incline unto, therein **the good** is his end. Wherein the end of every thing doth **of a** consist, therein also doth his good and benefit **rational** consist. Society therefore is the proper good of **creation** a rationall creature. For that we are made for society, it hath long since beene demonstrated. Or can any man make any question of this, that whatsoever is naturally worse and inferiour, is ordinarily subordinated to that which is better? and that those things that are best, are made one for another? And those things that have soules, are better then those that have none? and of those that have, those best that have rationall soules?

XVI. To desire things impossible is the part of a mad man. But it is a thing impossible, that wicked man should not commit some such things. Neither doth any thing happen to any man, which in the ordinary course of nature as naturall unto him doth not happen. Againe, the same things happen unto others also. And truly, if either he that is ignorant that such a thing hath happened unto him, or he that is ambitious to be commended for his magnanimitie, can be patient, and is not grieved: is it not a grievous thing, that either ignorance or a vain desire to please and to be commended, should bee more powerfull and effectual than true prudence? As for the things themselves, they touch not the soule, neither can they have any accesse unto it: neither can they of themselves any wayes either affect it, or move it. For she her self alone can affect and move her selfe, and according as the Dogmata and

Mankind is near to us for well-doing opinions are, which shee doth vouchsafe her selfe, so are those things which, as accessories, have any coexistence with her.

XVII. After one consideration, man is neerest unto us; as we are bound to doe them good, and to beare with them. But as he may oppose any of our true proper actions, so man is unto me but as a thing indifferent: even as the sunne, or the winde, or some wilde beast. By some of these it may be, that some operation or other of mine, may be hindered; however, of my minde and resolution it selfe, there can be no let or impediment, by reason of that ordinary constant both Exception (or Reservation wherewith it inclineth) and ready Conversion of objects; from that which may not be, to that which may be, which in the prosecution of its inclinations, as occasion serves, it doth observe. For by these the minde doth turne and convert any impediment whatsoever, to be her aime and purpose. So that what before was the impediment, is now the principall object of her working; and that which before was in her way, is now her readiest way.

XVIII. Honour that which is chiefest and most powerfull in the world, and that is it, which makes use of all things, and governes all things. So also in thy selfe, honour that which is chiefest, and most powerfull; and is of one kinde and nature with that which we now spake of. For it is the very same, which being in thee, turneth all other things to its own use, and by whom also thy life is governed.

XIX. That which doth not hurt the Citie

it selfe, cannot hurt any Citizen. **This** rule thou must remember to apply and make use of upon every conceit and apprehension of wrong. If the whole Citie be not hurt by this, neither am I certainly. And if the whole be not, why should I make it my private grievance? consider rather what it is wherein he is overseen that is thought to have done the wrong. Againe, often meditate **how** swiftly all things that subsist, and all things that are done in the world, are carryed away, and as it were conveighed out of sight: For both the substances themselves, (we see) as a flood, are in a continuall fluxe; and all actions in a perpetuall change; and the causes themselves, subject to a thousand alterations, neither is there any thing almost, that may ever be said to be now setled, and constant. Next unto this, and which followes upon it, consider both the infinitenesse of the time already passed, and the immense vastnesse of that which is **to come,** wherein all things are to bee resolved and annihilated. Art not thou then a very foole, who **for** these things, art either puffed up with pride, or distracted with cares, or canst find in thy heart to make such moanes as for a thing that would trouble thee for a very long time? Consider the whole Universe, whereof thou art but a very little part, and the whole age of the world together, whereof but a short and very momentarie portion is allotted unto thee, and all the Fates and Destinies together, of which how much is it that comes to thy part and share! Againe: Another doth trespasse against **me.**

What hurts not the State, hurts not thee

<small>*What is it to live with the Gods?*</small> Let him looke to that. Hee is master of his owne disposition, and of his owne operation. I for my part am in the meane time in possession of as much, as the common Nature would have me to possesse: and that which mine owne Nature would have me doe, I doe.

XX. Let not that chiefe commanding part of thy soule bee ever subject to any variation through any corporall either paine or pleasure, neither suffer it to be mixed with these, but let it both circumscribe its selfe, and confine those affections to their owne proper parts and members. But if at any time they doe reflect, and rebound upon the mind and understanding (as in an united and compacted body it must needs;) then must thou not goe about to resist sense and feeling, it being naturall. However let not thy understanding to this naturall sense and feeling, which whether unto our flesh pleasant or painefull, is unto us nothing properly, adde an opinion of either good or bad, and all is well.

XXI. To live with the Gods. Hee liveth with the Gods, who at all times affords unto them the spectacle of a soule, both contented and well pleased with whatsoever is afforded, or allotted unto her; and performing whatsoever is pleasing to that Spirit, whom (being part of himselfe) Jove hath appointed to every man as his overseer and governour.

XXII. Bee not angry neither with him whose breath, neither with him whose *alæ*, or arme holes, are offensive. What can hee doe? such is his breath naturally, and such are his *ala*; and from such, such an effect, and such a smell must of necessity proceed. O, but the man (sayest thou) hath understanding in him, and might of himselfe know, that hee by standing neere, cannot choose but offend. And thou also (God blesse thee!) hast understanding. Let thy reasonable facultie, worke upon his reasonable facultie; shew him his fault, admonish him. If hee hearken unto thee, thou hast cured him, and there will be no more occasion of anger.

A true Retreat

XXIII. 'Where there shall neither roarer be, nor harlot.' Why so? As thou dost purpose to liue, when thou hast retyred thy selfe to some such place, where neither roarer, nor harlot is: so mayest thou here. And if they will not suffer thee, then maist thou leave thy life rather then thy calling, but so as one that doth not thinke himselfe any waies wronged. Only as one would say, Here is a smoake; I will out of it. And what a great matter is this? Now till some such thing force me out, I will continue free; neither shall any man hinder mee to doe what I will, and my will shall ever be by the proper nature of a reasonable and sociable creature, regulated and directed.

XXIV. That rationall essence by which the Universe is governed, is for communitie and societie; and therefore hath it both made the things that are worse, for the best, and hath allied and knit together those which are best, as it were in an harmonie. Seest thou not how it hath subordinated, and co-ordinated? and how it

True Magnanimity hath distributed unto every thing according to its worth? and those which have the præeminencie and superioritie aboue all, hath it united together, into a mutuall consent and agreement.

XXV. How hast thou carried thy selfe hitherto towards the Gods? towards thy Parents? towards thy Brethren? towards thy Wife? towards thy Children? towards thy Masters? thy foster Fathers? thy Friends? thy Domesticks? thy Servants? Is it so with thee, that hitherto thou hast neither by worde or deed wronged any of them? Remember withall through how many things thou hast already passed, and how many thou hast beene able to endure; so that now the Legend of thy life is full, and thy charge is accomplished. Againe, how many truly good things have certainely by thee beene discerned? how many pleasures, how many paines hast thou passed over with contempt? how many things externally glorious hast thou despised? towards how many perverse unreasonable men, hast thou carried thy selfe kindly, and discreetly?

XXVI. Why should imprudent unlearned soules trouble that which is both learned, and prudent? And which is that that is so? she that understandeth the beginning and the end, and hath the true knowledge of that Rationall essence, that passeth through all things subsisting, and through all ages being ever the same, disposing and dispensing as it were this Universe by certaine periods of time.

XXVII. Within a very little while, thou wilt

be either ashes, or a sceletum ; and a Name per- *What is*
chance ; and perchance, not so much as a Name. *a Name?*
And what is that but an empty sound, and a rebounding Eccho? Those things which in this life are deerest unto us, and of most account, they are in themselves but vaine, putrid, contemptible. The most waighty and serious, if rightly esteemed, but as puppies, biting one another : or untoward children, now laughing and then crying. As for faith, and modesty, and justice, and truth, they long since, as one of the Poets hath it, have abandoned this spacious Earth, and retired themselves unto Heaven. What is it then that doth keepe thee here, if things sensible bee so mutable and unsettled? and the senses so obscure, and so fallible? and our soules nothing but an exhalation of blood? and to be in credit among such, be but vanity? What is it that thou dost stay for? an Extinction, or a Translation; either of them with a propitious and contented mind. But till that time come, what will content thee? what else, but to worship and praise the Gods ; and to doe good unto men. To beare with them, and to forbeare to doe them any wrong. And for all externall things belonging either to this thy wretched body, or life, to remember that they are neither thine, nor in thy power.

XXVIII. Thou mayest alwayes speed, if thou wilt but make choise of the right way ; if in the course both of thine opinions and actions, thou wilt observe a true method. These two things be common to the soules, as of God, so

Be not carried away by common opinion of men, and of every reasonable creature, first that in their owne proper worke they cannot be hindered by any thing: and secondly, that their happinesse doth consist in a disposition to, and in the practise of righteousnesse; and that in these their desire is terminated.

XXIX. If this neither be my wicked act, nor an act any wayes depending from any wickednesse of mine, and that by it the publike is not hurt; what doth it concerne me? And wherein can the publike be hurt? For thou must not altogether be carryed by conceit and common opinion: as for help thou must afford that unto them after thy best ability, and as occasion shall require, though they sustaine dammage, but in these middle or worldly things; but however doe not thou conceive that they are truly hurt thereby: for that is not right. But as that old foster Father in the Comædie, being now to take his leave doth with a great deale of Ceremonie, require his Foster Childs rhombus, or rattle-top, remembring neverthelesse that it is but a rhombus; so here also do thou likewise. For indeed what is all this pleading and publick bawling for at the Courts? O man, hast thou forgotten what those things are! yea but they are things that others much care for, and highly esteeme of. Wilt thou therefore be a foole too? Once I was; let that suffice.

XXX. Let death surprise me when it will, and where it will, I may bee εὔμοιρος, or a happy man, neverthelesse. For he is a happy man, who in his life time dealeth unto himselfe a

happy lot and portion. A happy lot and portion Care not
is, good inclinations of the soule, good desires, for praise
good actions. or blame

The Sixth Booke

THE matter it selfe, of which the Universe doth consist, is of it selfe very tractable and pliable. That rationall essence that doth governe it, hath in it selfe no cause to doe evill. It hath no evill in it selfe neither can it doe any thing that is evill: neither can any thing be hurt by it. And all things are done and determined according to its will and prescript.

II. Bee it all one unto thee, whether halfe frozen or well warme; whether only slumbering or after a full sleepe; whether discommended or commended thou doe thy duty: or whether dying or doing somewhat else; for that also 'to die,' must among the rest be reckoned as one of the duties and actions of our lives.

III. Looke in, let not either the proper qualitie, or the true worth of any thing passe thee, before thou hast fully apprehended it.

IV. All substances, come soone to their change, and either they shall be resolved by way of exhalation (if so be that all things shall bee reunited into one substance), or as others maintaine, they shall be scattered and dispersed. As for that Rationall Essence by which all things are governed, as it best understandeth it selfe, both its owne disposition, and what it

True revenge doth, and what matter it hath to doe with and accordingly doth all things; so we that do not, no wonder, if wee wonder at many things, the reasons whereof we cannot comprehend.

V. The best kinde of revenge is, not to become like unto them.

VI. Let this be thy only joy, and thy only comfort, from one sociable kinde action without intermission to passe unto another, God being ever in thy minde.

VII. The rationall commanding part, as it alone can stirre up and turne it selfe; so it maketh both it selfe to be, and every thing that happeneth, to appeare unto it selfe, as it will it selfe.

VIII. According to the nature of the Universe all things particular are determined, not according to any other nature, either about compassing and containing; or within, dispersed and contained; or without, depending. Either this Universe is a meere confused masse, and an intricate context of things, which shall in time be scattered and dispersed againe: or it is an Union consisting of Order, and administred by providence. If the first, why should I desire to continue any longer in this fortuit confusion and commixtion? or why should I take care for any thing else, but that as soon as may be I may be Earth againe? And why should I trouble my selfe any more whilest I seeke to please the gods? Whatsoever I doe, Dispersion is my end, and will come upon me whether I will or noe. But if the latter be, then am not I religious in vaine;

then will I be quiet and patient, and put my trust in Him, who is the Governor of all.

Be still and trust in God

IX. Whensoever by some present hard occurrences thou art constrained to be in some sort troubled and vexed, returne unto thy selfe as **soone** as may be, and be not out of tune longer then thou must needs. For so shalt thou be the better able to keepe thy part another time, and to maintaine the harmonie, if thou doest use thy selfe to this continually; once out, presently to have recourse unto it, and to beginne againe.

X. If it were that thou hadst at one time both a stepmother, and a naturall mother living, thou wouldest honour and respect her also; neverthelesse to thine owne naturall mother would thy refuge, **and** recourse be continually. So let the Court and thy Philosophie be unto thee. Have **recourse** unto it often, and comfort thy selfe in her, by whom it is that those other things are made tolerable unto thee, and thou also in those things not intolerable unto others.

XI. How marvellous usefull it is for a man to represent unto himselfe meates, and all such things that are for the mouth, under a right apprehension **and** imagination! as for example: This is the carkase of a fish; this of a bird; and this of a hogge. And againe more generally; This Phalernum, this excellent highly commended wine, is but the bare juyce of an ordinary grape. This purple robe, but sheepes haires, dyed with the blood of a shell-fish. So for coitus, it is but the attrition of an ordinarie base entrall, and the excretion of a little vile snivell, with a certaine kinde of con-

Things admired vulsion: according to Hippocrates his opinion. How excellent usefull are these lively phancies and representations of things, thus penetrating and passing through the objects, to make their true nature knowne and apparant! This must thou use all thy life long, and upon all occasions: and then especially, when matters are apprehended as of great worth and respect, thy art and care must be to uncover them, and to behold their vilenesse, and to take away from them all those serious circumstances and expressions, under which they made so grave a shew. For outward pompe and appearance, is a great jugler; and then especially art thou most in danger to be beguiled by it, when (to a mans thinking) thou most seemest to be imployed about matters of moment.

XII. See what Crates pronounceth concerning Xenocrates himselfe.

XIII. Those things which the common sort of people doe admire, are most of them such things as are very generall, and may be comprehended under things meerely naturall, or naturally affected and qualified: as stones, wood, figs, vines, olives. Those that be admired by them that are more moderate and restrained, are comprehended under things animated: as flocks and heards. Those that are yet more gentile and curious, their admiration is commonly confined to reasonable creatures only; not in generall as they are reasonable, but as they are capable of art, or of some craft and subtile invention: or perchance barely to reasonable creatures; as they that delight in the possession of many slaves.

But he that honours a reasonable soule in generall, as it is reasonable and naturally sociable, doth little regard any thing else: and above all things is carefull to preserve his owne, in the continuall habit and exercise both of reason and sociablenesse: and thereby doth co-operate with him, of whose nature hee doth also participate; God.

Change and decay

XIV. Some things hasten to be, and others to be no more. And even whatsoever now is, some part thereof hath already perished. Perpetuall fluxes and alterations renew the world, as the perpetuall course of time doth make the age of the world (of it selfe infinite) to appeare alwaies fresh and new. In such a fluxe and course of all things, what of these things that hasten so fast away should any man regard, since among all there is not any that a man may fasten and fixe upon? as if a man would settle his affection upon some ordinary sparrow flying by him, who is no sooner seene, then out of sight. For wee must not thinke otherwise of our lives, then as a meere exhalation of blood, or of an ordinary respiration of aire. For what in our common apprehension is, to breath in the aire and to breath it out againe, which wee doe daily: so much is it and no more, at once to breath out all thy respirative facultie into that common aire from whence but lately (as being but from yesterday, and to-day), thou didst first breath it in, and with it, life.

XV. Not vegetative spiration, it is not surely (which plants have) that in this life should bee

What should be dear unto thee so deare unto us; nor sensitive respiration, the proper life of beasts, both tame and wild; nor this our imaginative faculty; nor that wee are subject to be led and carried up and downe by the strength of our sensuall appetites; or that wee can gather, and live together; or that wee can feed: for that in effect is no better, than that wee can void the excrements of our food. What is it then that should be deare unto us? to heare a clattering noise? if not that, then neither to be applauded by the tongues of men. For the praises of many tongues, is in effect no better, then the clattering of so many tongues. If then neither applause, what is there remaining that should be deare unto thee? This I thinke: that in all thy motions and actions thou be moved, and restrained according to thine owne true naturall constitution and construction only. And to this even ordinary arts and professions doe lead us. For it is that which every art doth ayme at, that whatsoever it is, that is by art effected and prepared, may be fit for that worke that it is prepared for. This is the end that he that dresseth the vine, and he that takes upon him either to tame colts, or to traine up dogs, doth ayme at. What else doth the education of Children, and all learned professions tend unto? Certainly then it is that, which should be deare unto us also. If in this particular it goe well with thee, care not for the obteining of other things. But is it so, that thou canst not but respect other things also? Then canst not thou truely be free; then canst thou not have selfe content: then wilt thou ever be subject to passions. For it is not possible, but that thou must be envious, and jealous, and suspitious of them who thou knowest can bereaue thee of such things; and againe, a secret underminer of them, whom thou seest in present possession of that which is deare unto thee. To be short, he must of necessity be full of confusion within himselfe, and often accuse the Gods, whosoever stands in neede of these things. But if tnou shalt honour and respect thy mind only, that will make thee acceptable towards thy selfe, towards thy friends very tractable; and conformable and concordant with the Gods; that is, accepting with praises whatsoever they shall thinke good to appoint and allot unto thee.

How to be content

XVI. Under, above, and about, are the motions of the Elements; but the motion of vertue, is none of those motions, but is somewhat more excellent and divine. Whose way (to speed and prosper in it) must be through a way, that is not easily comprehended.

XVII. Who can choose but wonder at them? They will not speake well of them that are at the same time with them, and live with them; yet they themselves are very ambitious, that they that shall follow, whom they have never seene, nor shall ever see, should speake well of them. As if a man should grieve that he hath not beene commended by them, that lived before him.

XVIII. Doe not ever conceive any thing impossible to man, which by thee cannot, or

How to keep a calm temper not without much difficultie be effected; but whatsoever in generall thou canst conceive possible and proper unto any man, thinke that very possible unto thee also.

XIX. Suppose that at the Palæstra some body hath all to-torne thee with his nailes, and hath broken thy head. Well, thou art wounded. Yet thou dost not exclaime; thou **art not** offended with him. Thou dost not suspect him for it afterwards, as one that watcheth to doe thee a mischiefe. Yea even then, though thou dost thy best to save thy selfe from him, yet not from him as an enemy. It is not by way of any suspitious indignation, but by way of gentle and friendly declination. Keepe the same mind and disposition in other parts of thy life also. For many things there be, which **wee** must conceit and apprehend, as though wee had had to doe with an antagonist at the Palæstra. For as I said, it is very possible for us to avoid and decline, though we neyther suspect, nor hate.

XX. If any body shall reprove me, and shall make it apparant unto me, that in any either opinion or action of mine I doe erre, I will most gladly retract. For it is the truth that I seeke after, by which I am sure that never any man was hurt; and as sure, that he is hurt that continueth in any error, or ignorance whatsoever.

XXI. I for my part will doe what belongs unto mee; as for other things, whether things unsensible or things irrationall; or if rationall, yet deceived and ignorant of the true way, they shall not trouble or distract mee. For as for those creatures which are not indued with reason, and all other things and matters of the world whatsoever, I freely, and generously, as one endued with reason, of things that have none, make use of them. And as for men, towards them as naturally partakers of the same reason, my care is to carry my selfe sociably. But whatsoever it is that thou art about, remember to call upon the Gods. And as for the time how long thou shalt live to do these things, let it be altogether indifferent unto thee, for even three such houres are sufficient.

All come to dust

XXII. Alexander of Macedon, and he that dressed his mules, when once dead both came to one. For either they were both resumed into those originall rationall essences from whence all things in the world are propagated; or both after one fashion were scattered into Atomes.

XXIII. Consider how many different things, whether they concerne our bodies, or our soules, in a moment of time come to passe in every one of us, and so thou wilt not wonder if many more things or rather all things that are done, can at one time subsist, and coexist in that both One and Generall, which wee call the World.

XXIV. If any should put this question unto thee, how this word Antoninus is written, wouldest thou not presently fixe thine intention upon it, and utter out in order every letter of it? And if any shall beginne to gainesay thee, and quarrell with thee about it; wilt thou quarrell with him againe, or rather goe on meekly as thou hast begun, untill thou hast numbred out every letter? Here then likewise remember, that every duty that belongs unto a man doth consist of some certaine letters or numbers as it were, to which without any noise or tumult keeping thy selfe, thou must orderly proceed to thy proposed end, forbearing to quarrell with him that would quarrell and fall out with thee.

Death or release

XXV. Is it not a cruell thing to forbid men to affect those things, which they conceive to agree best with their owne natures, and to tend most to their owne proper good and behoofe? But thou after a sort deniest them this libertie, as often as thou art angry with them for their sins. For surely they are led unto those sins whatsoever they be, as to their proper good and commoditie. But it is not so (thou wilt object perchance). Thou therefore teach them better, and make it appeare unto them: but be not thou angry with them.

XXVI. Death is a cessation from the impressions of the senses, the tyranny of the passions, the errors of the minde, and the servitude of the body.

XXVII. If in this kinde of life thy body be able to hold out, it is a shame that thy soule should faint first, and give over. Take heed, lest of a Philosopher thou become a meere Cæsar in time, and receive a new tincture from the Court. For it may happen if thou dost not take heed. Keepe thy selfe therefore, truly simple, good, sincere, grave, free from all ostentation, a lover of that which is just, religious,

kinde, tender hearted, strong and vigorous to **A model**
undergoe any thing that becomes thee. En- **Prince**
deavour to continue such, as philosophie (hadst
thou wholly and constantly applyed thy selfe
unto it) would have made, and secured thee.
Worship the gods, procure the welfare **of** men,
this life is short. Charitable actions, and a holy
disposition, is the onely fruit of this earthly life.

XXVIII. Doe all things as becommeth the
Disciple of Antoninus Pius. Remember his
resolute constancie in things that were done by
him according to reason, his equability in all
things, his sanctity; the cheerefulnesse of his
countenance, his sweetnesse, and how free hee
was from all vaine glory; how carefull to come
to the true and exact knowledge of matters in
hand, and how hee would by no meanes give
over till he did fully, and plainely understand
the whole state of the businesse; and how
patiently, and without any contestation he would
beare with them, that did unjustly condemne
him: how he would never be overhasty in any
thing, nor give eare to slanders and false accusations, but examine and observe with best dili-
gence the severall actions **and** dispositions of
men. Againe, how hee was no backbiter, nor
easily frighted, nor suspicious, and in his language
free from all affectation and curiosity: and how
easily hee would content himselfe with few
things, as lodging, bedding, cloathing, and
ordinarie nourishment, and attendance. How
able to endure labour, how patient; able through
his spare dyet to continue from morning to even-

Look on the world as on a dream

ing without any necessity of withdrawing before his accustomed houres to the necessities **of** nature: his uniformity and constancie in matter of friendship. How he would beare with them that with all boldnesse and libertie opposed his opinions; and even rejoyce if any man could better advise him: and lastly, how religious hee was without superstition. All these things of him remember, that whensoever thy last houre shal come upon thee, it may find thee, as it did him, ready for it in the possession of **a good** conscience.

XXIX. Stirre up thy minde, and recall thy wits againe from thy naturall dreames, and visions, and when thou art perfectly awaken, and canst perceive that they were but dreames that troubled thee, as one newly awakened out of another kinde of sleepe looke upon these worldly things with the same minde as thou didst upon those, that thou sawest in thy sleepe.

XXX. I consist of body and soule, unto my body all things are indifferent, for of it selfe it cannot affect one thing more then another with apprehension of any difference; as for my mind, all things which are not within the verge of her owne operation, are indifferent unto her, and for her owne operations, those altogether depend of her; neither doth she busie her selfe about any, but those that are present; for as for future and passed operations, those also are now at this present indifferent unto her.

XXXI. As long as the foot doth that which belongeth unto it to doe, and the hand that which belongs unto it, their labour, whatsoever it be, **The true** is not unnaturall. So a man as long as he doth **nature** that which is proper unto a man, his labour can- **of man** not be against nature; and if it be not against nature, then neither is it hurtfull unto him. But if it were so that happinesse did consist in pleasure: how came notorious robbers, impure abominable livers, parricides, and tyrants, in so large a measure to have their part of pleasures?

XXXII. Doest thou not see, how even those that professe mechanique arts, though in some respect they be no better then meere Idiots, yet they stick close to the course of their trade, neither can they finde in their heart to decline from it, and is it not a grievous thing that an architect, or a physitian shall respect the course and mysteries of their profession, more then a man the proper course and condition of his owne nature, Reason, which is common to him and to the gods?

XXXIII. Asia, Europe; what are they, but as corners of the whole world; of which the whole Sea, is but as one drop; and the great mount Athos, but as a clodde, as all present time is but as one point of eternity. All, petty things; all things that are soone altered, soone perished. And all things come from one beginning; either all severally and particularly deliberated and resolved upon, by the generall ruler and governour of all; or all by necessary consequence. So that the dreadfull hiatus of a gaping Lion, and all poyson, and all hurtfull things, are but (as the thorn and the myre) the

Fit thyself to thy fate necessary consequences of goodly faire things. Think not of these therefore, as things contrary to those which thou doest much honour, and respect; but consider in thy minde the **true** fountaine of all.

XXXIV. Hee that seeth the things that are now, hath seene all that either was ever, or ever shall be, for all things are of one kinde; and all like one unto another. Meditate often upon the connexion of all things in the world; and upon the mutuall relation that they have one unto another. For all things are after a sort folded and involved one within another, and by these meanes all agree well together. For one thing is consequent unto another, by locall motion, by naturall conspiration and agreement, and by substantiall union, or, reduction of all substances into One.

XXXV. Fit and accommodate thy selfe to that estate and to those occurrences, which by the destinies have beene annexed unto thee; and love those men whom thy fate it is to li**ve with**; but love them truly. An instrument, a toole, an utensile, whatsoever it be, if it be fit for the purpose it was made for, it is as it should be, though he perchance that made and fitted it, be out of sight and gone. But in things naturall, that power which hath framed and fitted them, is and abideth within them still: for which reason shee ought also the more to be respected, and **wee are** the more obliged (if wee may live and passe our time according to her purpose and intention) to thinke that all is well with us, and according to our owne mindes. After this manner also, and in this respect it is, that He that is all in all doth enjoy his happinesse.

No need for murmuring

XXXVI. What things soever are not within the proper power and jurisdiction of thine owne will either to compasse or avoid, if thou shalt propose unto thy selfe any of those things as either good, or evill; it must needs be that according as thou shalt either fall into that which thou doest thinke evill, or misse of that which thou doest thinke good, so wilt thou be ready both to complaine of the gods, and to hate those men, who either shall be so indeed, or shall by thee be suspected as the cause either of thy missing of the one, or falling into the other. And indeed we must needs commit many evills, if wee incline to any of these things, more or lesse, with an opinion of any difference. But if we minde and phancie those things only, as good and bad, which wholly depend of our owne wills, there is no more occasion why we should either murmur against the gods, or be at enmitie with any man.

XXXVII. Wee all worke to one effect, some willingly, and with a rationall apprehension of what we doe: others without any such knowledge. As I thinke Heraclitus in a place speaketh of them that sleepe, that even they doe worke in their kinde, and doe conferre to the generall operations of the World. One man therefore doth cooperate after one sort, and another after another sort; but even he that doth murmur, and to his power doth resist and

Thy life must serve God's ends hinder; even he as much as any doth cooperate. For of such also did the World stand in need. Now doe thou consider among which of these thou wilt ranke thy selfe. For as for him who is the Administrator of all, he will make good use of thee whether thou wilt or no, and make thee (as a part and member of the whole) so to cooperate with him, that whatsoever thou doest, shall turne to the furtherance of his owne counsells, and resolutions. But be not thou for shame such a part of the whole, as that vile and ridiculous verse (which Chrysippus in a place doth mention) is a part of the Comædy.

XXXVIII. Doth either the Sunne take upon him to doe that which belongs to the raine? or his son Æsculapius that, which unto the Earth doth properly belong? How is it with every one of the starres in particular? Though they all differ one from another, and have their severall charges and functions by themselves, doe they not all neverthelesse concurre and cooperate to one end?

XXXIX. If so be that the gods have deliberated in particular of those things that should happen unto me, I must stand to their deliberation, as discreet and wise. For that a god should be an imprudent god, is a thing hard even to conceive: and why should they resolve to do me hurt? for what profit either unto them or the universe (which they specially take care for) could arise from it? But if so be that they have not deliberated of me in particular, certainly they have of the whole in generall, and those things which in consequence and coherence of this generall deliberation happen unto me in particular, I am bound to embrace and accept of. But if so be that they have not deliberated at all (which indeed is very irreligious for any man to beleeve: for then let us neither sacrifice, nor pray, nor respect our oaths, neither let us any more use any of those things, which we perswaded of the presence and secret conversation of the gods among us, daily use and practise:) but, I say, if so be that they have not indeed either in generall, or particular deliberated of any of those things, that happen unto us in this world; yet God be thanked, that of those things that concerne my selfe, it is lawfull for me to deliberate my selfe, and all my deliberation is but concerning that which may be to me most profitable. Now that unto every one is most profitable, which is according to his owne constitution and Nature. And my Nature is, to be rationall in all my actions and as a good, and naturall member of a citty and common wealth, towards my fellow members ever to be sociably and kindly disposed and affected. My City and Country as I am Antoninus, is Rome; as a man, the whole world. Those things therefore that are expedient and profitable to those Cities, are the onely things that are good and expedient for me.

My City is the World

XL. Whatsoever in any kind doth happen to any one, is expedient to the whole. And thus much to content us might suffice, that it is expedient for the whole in generall. But yet this

The long roll of the dead also shalt thou generally perceive, if thou dost diligently take heed, that whatsoever doth happen to any one man or men. . . . And now I am content that the word expedient, should more generally be understood of those things which wee otherwise call middle things, or, things indifferent; as health, wealth, and the like.

XLI. As the ordinary shewes of the Theatre and of other such places, when thou art presented with them, affect thee; as the same things still seene, and in the same fashion, make the sight ingratefull and tedious; so must all the things that wee see all our life long affect us. For all things, above and below, are still the same, and from the same causes. When then will there be an end?

XLII. Let the severall deaths of men of all sorts, and of all sorts of professions, and of all sort of nations, be a perpetuall object of thy thoughts, . . . so that thou mayst even come downe to Philistio, Phœbus, and Origanion. Passe now to other generations. Thither shall wee after many changes, where so many brave Oratours are; where so many grave Philosophers; Heraclitus, Pythagoras, Socrates. Where so many Heroes of the old times; and then so many brave captaines of the latter times; and so many Kings. After all these, where Eudoxus, Hipparchus, Archimedes; where so many other sharpe, generous, industrious, subtile, peremptory dispositions; and among others, even they, that have beene the greatest scoffers and deriders of the frailty and brevity of this our humane life;

as Menippus, and others, as many as there have beene such as hee. Of all these consider, that they long since are all dead, and gone. And what doe they suffer by it! Nay they that have not so much as a Name remaining, what are they the worse for it? One thing there is, and that onely, which is worth our while in this World, and ought by us much to be esteemed; and that is, according to truth and righteousnesse, meekely and lovingly to converse with false, and unrighteous men.

Look on the virtues of your friends

XLIII. When thou wilt comfort and cheare thy selfe, call to mind the severall gifts and vertues of them, whom thou dost daily converse with; as for example, the industry of the one; the modestie of another; the liberality of a third; of another some other thing. For nothing can so much rejoyce thee, as the resemblances and parallels of severall vertues, visible and eminent in the dispositions of those who live with thee; especially when, all at once, as neere as may be, they represent themselves unto thee. And therefore thou must have them alwaies in a readinesse.

XLIV. Dost thou grieve that thou dost weigh but so many pounds, and not 300 rather? Iust as much reason hast thou to grieve that thou must live but so many yeares, and not longer. For as for bulcke and substance thou dost content thy selfe with that proportion of it that is allotted unto thee, so shouldst thou for time.

XLV. Let us doe our best endeavours to

True happiness in thy own action

perswade them; but however, if Reason and Justice lead thee to it, doe it, though they be never so much against it. But if any shall by force withstand thee, and hinder thee in it, convert thy vertuous inclination from one object unto another, from Iustice to contented æquanimity, and chearfull patience: so that what in the one is thy hinderance, thou mayest make use of it for the exercise of another vertue: and remember that it was with due exception, and reservation, that thou didst at first incline and desire. For thou didst not set thy mind upon things impossible. Upon what then? that all thy desires might ever be moderated with this due kinde of reservation. And this thou hast, and mayst alwaies obtaine, whether the thing desired be in thy power or no. And what doe I care for more, if that for which I was borne, and brought forth into the world (to rule all my desires with reason and discretion) may be?

XLVI. The ambitious supposeth another mans act, praise and applause, to be his owne happinesse; the voluptuous his owne sense and feeling; but hee that is wise, his owne action.

XLVII. It is in thy power absolutely to exclude all manner of conceit and opinion, as concerning this matter; and by the same means, to exclude all griefe and sorrow from thy soule. For as for the things and objects themselves, they of themselves have no such power, whereby to beget and force upon us any opinion at all.

XLVIII. Use thy selfe when any man speaks unto thee, so to hearken unto him, as that in the interim, thou give not way to any other thoughts; that so thou **mayst** (as farre as is possible) **seeme** fixed and fastned to his very **soule,** whosoever he be that speakes unto thee.

Why should I be angry at trifles?

XLIX. That which is not good for the Bee hive, cannot be good for the Bee.

L. Will either passengers, or patients, finde fault and complaine, either the one if they be well **carried, or** the others if well cured? Doe they take **care** for any more then this; the one, that their Shipmaster may bring them safe to land, and the other, that their Physitian may effect their recovery.

LI. How many of them who came into the world at the same time when I did, are already **gone out** of it?

LII. To them that are sick of the jaundis, honie seemes bitter; and to them that are bitten by a mad dogge, the water terrible; and to children, a little ball seemes a fine thing. And why then should I be angry? or doe I thinke that error and false opinion is lesse powerfull to **make men** transgresse, then either choler, being immoderate and excessive, to cause the jaundis; or poyson, to cause rage?

LIII. No man can hinder thee to live as thy **nature** doth require. Nothing can happen unto thee, but what the common good of Nature doth require.

LIV. What manner of men they be whom they seeke to please, and what to get, and by what actions: how soone time will cover and

My mind is in my own power

burie all things and how many it hath already buryed!

The Seventh Booke

WHAT is wickedness? It is that which many times and often thou hast already seene and knowne in the world. And so oft as anything doth happen that might otherwise trouble thee, let this memento presently come to thy mind, that it is that which thou hast already often seene and knowne. Generally, above and below, thou shalt find but the same things. The very same things whereof ancient stories, middle age stories, and fresh stories are full: whereof towns are full, and houses full. There is nothing that is new. All things that are, are both usuall and of little continuance.

II. What feare is there that thy Dogmata, or Philosophicall resolutions and conclusions, should become dead in thee, and lose their proper power and efficacie to make thee live happy, as long as those proper and correlative phancies, and representations of things on which they mutually depend (which continually to stirre up and revive is in thy power,) are still kept fresh and alive? It is in my power concerning this thing that is happened, whatsoever it be, to conceit that which is right and true. If it be, why then am I troubled? Those things that are without my understanding, are nothing to it at all: and that is it only, which doth properly concerne me. Be alwayes in this minde, and thou wilt be right.

The great puppet show

III. That which most men would thinke themselves most happy for, and would preferre before all things, if the gods would grant it unto them after their deaths, thou mayest whilest thou livest grant unto thy selfe; to live againe. See the things of the world againe; as thou hast already seene them. For what is it else to live againe? Publick shewes and solemnities with much pompe and vanitie, stage playes, flocks and heards; conflicts and contentions: a bone throwne to a companie of hungry curres; a bait for greedy fishes; the painefulnesse, and continuall burden-bearing of wretched ants, the running to and fro of terrified myce: little puppets drawne up and downe with wyres and nerves: these bee the objects of the World. Among all these thou must stand stedfast, meekly affected, and free from all manner of indignation; with this right ratiocination and apprehension; that as the worth is of those things which a man doth affect, so is in very deed every mans worth more or lesse.

IV. Word after word, every one by it selfe, must the things that are spoken be conceived and understood; and so the things that are done, purpose after purpose, every one by it selfe likewise. And as in matter of purposes and actions, wee must presently see what is the proper use and relation of every one; so of words must we be as ready, to consider of every one what is the true meaning, and signification of it according

Despise not the help of others to truth and Nature, however it be taken in common use.

V. Is my reason, and understanding sufficient for this, or no? If it be sufficient, without any private applause, or publick ostentation as of an Instrument, which by nature I am provided of, I will make use of it for the worke in hand, as of an Instrument, which by nature I am provided of. If it be not, and that otherwise it belong not unto me particularly as a private duty, I will either give it over, and leave it to some other that can better effect it: or I will endeavour it; but with the helpe of some other, who with the joynt helpe of my reason, is able to bring somewhat to passe, that will now be seasonable and useful for the common good. For whatsoever I doe either by my selfe, or with some other, the only thing that I must intend, is, that it be good and expedient for the publick. For as for praise, consider how many who once were much commended, are now already quite forgotten, yea they that commended them, how even they themselves are long since dead and gone. Be not therefore ashamed, whensoever thou must use the helpe of others. For whatsoever it be, that lyeth upon thee to effect, thou must propose it unto thy selfe, as the scaling of wals is unto a soldier. And what if thou through either lamenesse or some other impediment art not able to reach unto the top of the battlements alone, which with the helpe of another thou maiest; wilt thou therefore give it over, or goe about it with lesse courage and alacrity, because thou canst not effect it all alone?

VI. Let not things future trouble thee. For if necessity so require that they come to passe, thou shalt (whensoever that is) be provided for them with the same reason, by which whatsoever is now present, is made both tolerable and acceptable unto thee. All things are linked and knitted together, and the knot is sacred, neither is there any thing in the world, that is not kinde and naturall in regard of any other thing, or, that hath not some kinde of reference, and naturall correspondence with whatsoever is in the world besides. For all things are ranked together, and by that decency of its due place and order that each particular doth observe, they all concurre together to the making of one and the same Κόσμος or World: as if you said, a comely peece, or an orderly composition. For all things throughout, there is but one and the same order; and through all things, one and the same god, the same substance and the same Law. There is one common Reason, and one common Truth, that belongs unto all reasonable creatures, for neither is there save one perfection of all creatures that are of the same kinde, and partakers of the same reason. *One God, one Truth, one Reason*

VII. Whatsoever is materiall, doth soone vanish away into the common substance of the whole; and whatsoever is formall, or, whatsoever doth animate that which is materiall, is soone resumed into the common Reason of the Whole; and the fame and memorie of any thing, is soone swallowed up by the generall Age and duration of the whole.

To thy own self be true

VIII. To a reasonable creature, the same action is both according to nature, and according to reason.

IX. Straight of it selfe, not made straight.

X. As severall members in one body united, so are reasonable creatures in a body divided and dispersed, all made and prepared for one common operation. And this thou shalt apprehend the better, if thou shalt use thy selfe often to say to thy selfe, I am μέλος, or a member of the masse and body of reasonable substances. But if thou shalt say I am μέρος, or a part, thou doest not yet love men from thy heart. The joy that thou takest in the exercise of bountie, is not yet grounded upon a due ratiocination, and right apprehension of the nature of things. Thou doest exercise it as yet upon this ground barely, as a thing convenient and fitting; not, as doing good to thy selfe, when thou doest good unto others.

XI. Of things that are externall happen what will to that which can suffer by externall accidents. Those things that suffer let them complaine themselves, if they will; as for me, as long as I conceive no such thing, that that which is happened is evill, I have no hurt; and it is in my power not to conceive any such thing.

XII. Whatsoever any man either doth or saith, thou must be good; not for any man's sake, but for thine owne natures sake; as if either gold, or the Emrald, or purple, should ever be saying to themselves, Whatsoever any man either doth or saith, I must still be an Emrald, and I must keepe my colour.

Reason is sufficient unto herself

XIII. This may ever be my comfort and securitie: my understanding, that ruleth over all, will not of it selfe bring trouble and vexation upon it selfe. This I say; it will not put it selfe in any feare, it will not lead it selfe into any concupiscence. If it be in the power of any other to compell it to feare, or to grieve, it is free for him to use his power. But sure if it selfe doe not of it selfe, through some false opinion or supposition incline it selfe to any such disposition; there is no feare. For as for the body, why should I make the griefe of my body, to be the grief of my minde? If that it selfe can either feare or complaine, let it. But as for the soule, which indeed, can only be truly sensible of either feare or griefe; to which only it belongs according to its different imaginations and opinions, to admit of either of these, or of their contraries; thou mayest look to that thy selfe, that it suffer nothing. Induce her not to any such opinion or perswasion. The understanding is of it selfe sufficient unto it selfe, and needs not (if it selfe doth not bring it selfe to need) any other thing besides it selfe, and by consequent as it needs nothing, so neither can it be troubled or hindered by any thing, if it selfe doth not trouble and hinder it selfe.

XIV. What is εὐδαιμονία or, happinesse: but ἀγαθὸς δαίμων, or, a good Dæmon, or Spirit? What then doest thou doe here, O opinion? By the gods I adjure thee, that thou get thee gone, as

Universal change thou camest: for I need thee not. Thou camest indeed unto me according to thy ancient wonted manner. It is that, that all men have ever beene subject unto. That thou camest therefore I am not angry with thee, only be gone, now that I have found thee what thou art.

XV. Is any man so foolish as to feare change, to which all things that once were not owe their being? And what is it, that is more pleasing and more familiar to the nature of the Universe? How couldst thou thy selfe use thy ordinary hot bathes, should not the wood that heateth them first be changed? How couldest thou receive any nourishment from those things that thou hast eaten, if they should not be changed? Can any thing else almost (that is usefull and profitable) bee brought to passe without change? How then doest not thou perceive, that for thee also, by death, to come to change, is a thing of the very same nature, and as necessary for the nature of the Universe?

XVI. Through the Substance of the Universe, as through a torrent passe all particular bodies, being all of the same nature, and all joynt workers with the Universe it selfe, as in one of our bodies so many members among themselves. How many such as Chrysippus, how many such as Socrates, how many such as Epictetus, hath the Age of the world long since swallowed up and devoured? Let this, be it either men or businesses, that thou hast occasion to thinke of, to the end that thy thoughts be not distracted and thy minde too earnestly set upon any thing, upon every such occasion presently come to thy minde. **Love** Of all **my** thoughts and cares, one **only** thing shall **your** be the **object**, that I my selfe doe nothing which **enemies** to the proper constitution of man, (either in regard of the thing it selfe, or in regard of the manner, or of the time of doing,) is contrarie. The time when thou shalt have forgotten all things, is at hand. And that time also is at hand, when thou thy selfe shalt be forgotten by all. Whilest thou art, apply thy selfe to that especially which unto man **as he** is a man, is most proper and agreeable, and that **is**, for a man even to love them that transgresse against him. This shall be, if at the same time that any such thing doth happen, thou call to minde, that they are thy Kinsmen; that it is through ignorance and against their wills that they sinne; and that within a very short while after, both thou and he shall **be no** more. But above all things, that he hath not done thee any hurt; for that by him thy minde and understanding is not made worse or more vile then it was before.

XVII. The nature of the Universe, of the common substance of all things as it were of so much waxe hath **now** perchance formed a horse; and then, destroying that figure, hath new tempered and fashioned the matter of it into the form and substance of a tree: then that againe into the forme and substance of a man: and then that againe into some other. Now every one of these doth subsist but for a very little while. As for dissolution, if it be no grievous thing **to** the chest or trunk, to be joyned together;

Tout com- prendre c'est tout par- donner

why should it be more grievous to be put asunder?

XVIII. An angry countenance is much against nature, and it is oftentimes the proper countenance of them that are at the point of death. But were it so, that all anger and passion were so throughly quenched in thee, that it were altogether impossible to kindle it any more, yet herein must not thou rest satisfied, but further endeavour by good consequence of true ratiocination, perfectly to conceive and understand, that all anger and passion is against reason. For if thou shalt not be sensible of thine innocencie; if that also shall be gone from thee, the comfort of a good conscience, that thou doest all things according to reason: what shouldest thou live any longer for? All things that now thou seest, are but for a moment. That nature, by which all things in the world are administred, will soone bring change and alteration upon them, and then of their substances make other things like unto them: and then soone after others againe of the matter and substance of these: that so by these meanes, the world may still appeare fresh and new.

XIX. Whensoever any man doth trespasse against thee, presently consider with thy selfe what it was that he did suppose to be good, what to be evill, when he did trespasse. For this when thou knowest, thou wilt pitty him; thou wilt have no occasion either to wonder, or to be angry. For either thou thy selfe doest yet live in that error and ignorance, as that thou doest suppose either that very thing that he doth, or **With-** some other like worldly thing, to bee good; and **draw into** so thou art bound to pardon him if hee have **thyself** done that which thou in the like case wouldest have done thy selfe. Or if so be that thou doest not any more suppose the same things to be good or evill, that he doth; how canst thou but be gentle unto him that is in an error?

XX. Phancie not to **thy** selfe things future, as though they were present: but of those that are present, take some aside, that thou takest most benefit of, and consider of them particularly, how wonderfully thou wouldest want them, if they were not present. But take heed withall, least that whilest thou doest settle thy contentment in things present, thou grow in time so to overprize them, as that the want of them (whensoever it **shall** so fall out) should be a trouble and a vexation unto thee. Winde up thy selfe into thy selfe. Such is the Nature of thy reasonable commanding part, as that if it exercise justice, and have by that meanes tranquillity within it selfe, it doth rest fully satisfied with it selfe without any other thing.

XXI. Wipe off all opinion: stay the force and violence of unreasonable lusts and affections: Circumscribe the present time: Examine whatsoever it be that is happened, either to thy selfe or to another: Divide all present objects, either in that which is formall or materiall: thinke of the last houre. That which thy neighbour hath committed, where the guilt of it lyeth, there let it rest. Examine in order whatsoever is spoken.

All things are by law Let thy minde penetrate, both into the effects, and into the causes. Rejoyce thy selfe with true simplicity, and modesty; and that all middle things betweene vertue and vice are indifferent unto thee. Finally, Love mankinde; obey God.

XXII. All things (saith he) are by certaine order and appointment. And what if the Elements onely.... It will suffice to remember, that all things in generall are by certaine order and appointment: or if it be but few. ... And as concerning death, that either Dispersion, or the Atomes, or Annihilation, or Extinction, or Translation will insue. And as concerning paine, that that which is intolerable is soone ended by death; and that which holds long must needs be tolerable; and that the minde in the meane time (which is all in all) may by way of interclusion, or interception, by stopping all manner of commerce and sympathie with the bodie, still retaine its owne tranquillity. Thy understanding is not made worse by it. As for those parts that suffer, let them, if they can, declare their griefe themselves. As for praise and commendation, view their minde and understanding, what estate they are in; what kinde of things they flie, and what things they seeke after: and that as in the sea-side, whatsoever was before to be seene, is by the continuall succession of new heapes of sand cast up one upon another, soone hid and covered; so in this life, all former things by those which immediately succeed.

XXIII. Out of Plato. 'He then whose minde

is endowed with true magnanimitie, who hath
accustomed himselfe to the contemplation both of
all times, and of all things in generall ; can this
mortall life (thinkest thou) seeme any great
matter unto him? It is not possible ; answered
hee. Then neither will such a one account
death a grievous thing? By no meanes.'

Like a shock of corn fully ripe

XXIV. Out of Antisthenes. 'It is a princely
thing to doe well, and to be ill spoken of. It is
a shamefull thing that the face should be subject
unto the minde, to be put into what shape it
will, and to be dressed by it as it will ; and that
the minde should not bestow so much care upon
her selfe, as to fashion her selfe, and to dresse
her selfe as best becommeth her.'

XXV. Out of severall poets and Comicks. 'It
will but little availe thee, to turne thine anger and
indignation upon the things themselves that have
fallen crosse unto thee. For as for them, they
are not sensible of it, &c. Thou shalt but make
thy selfe a laughing stock ; both unto the gods and
men, &c. Our life is reaped like a ripe eare of
corne : one is yet standing and another is down, &c.
But if so be that I and my children be neglected
by the gods, there is some reason even for that,
&c. As long as right and equity is of my side,
&c. Not to lament with them, Not to tremble,
&c.'

XXVI. Out of Plato. 'My answer, full of
justice and equitie, should be this : Thy speech is
not right, O man ! if thou supposest that he that is
of any worth at all, should apprehend either life
or death, as a matter of great hazard and danger ;

A soldier at his post and should not make this rather his only **care, to** examine his owne actions, whether just or unjust: whether actions of a good, or of a wicked man, &c. For thus in very truth, stands the case, O yee men of Athens. What place or station soever a man either hath chosen to himselfe, judging it best for himselfe; or is by lawfull authoritie put and setled in, therein doe I thinke (all appearance of danger notwithstanding) that hee should continue, as one who feareth neither death, nor any thing else, so much as he feareth to commit any thing that is vicious and shamefull, &c. But, O noble Sir, consider I pray, whether true generositie and true happinesse, doe not consist in somewhat else rather, then in the preservation either of ours, or other mens lives. For it is not the part of a man that is a man indeed, to desire to live long or to make much of his life whilest he liveth: But rather (he that is such) will in these things wholly referre himselfe unto the gods, and beleeving that which every woman can tell him, that, no man can escape death; the only thing that he takes thought and care for is this, that what time he liveth, he may live as well and as vertuously as he can possibly, &c. To looke about, and with the eyes to follow the course of the starres and planets, as though thou wouldest runne with them; and to minde perpetually the severall changes of the Elements one into another. For such phancies and imaginations, help much to purge away, the drosse and filth of this our earthly life, &c.' That also is a fine passage of Plato's, where he speaketh of worldly things in these words: 'Thou must **The har-** also as from some higher place looke downe, as **mony of** it were upon the things of this world, as flocks, **Creation** armies, husband-mens labours, mariages, divorces, generations, deaths: the tumults of Courts and places of judicatures; desert places; the severall nations of Barbarians, publick festivals, mournings, faires, markets.' How all things upon Earth **are** pesle mesle; and how miraculously things **contrary one to** another, concurre to the beautie and perfection of **this** Universe.

XXVII. To looke backe upon things of former ages, as upon the manifold changes and conversions of severall Monarchies and commonwealths. We may also foresee things future, for they shall all be of the same kinde; neither **is it** possible that they should leave the tune, or breake the consort that is now begunne as it were, by these things that are now done and brought to passe in the World. It comes all to one therefore, whether a man be a spectator of the things of this life but fortie yeares, or whether he see them ten thousand yeares together: for what shall he see more? 'And as for those parts that came from the Earth, they shall returne unto the Earth againe; and those that came from Heaven, they also shall returne unto those heavenly places.' **Whether** it be a meere dissolution and unbinding of the manifold intricacies and intanglements of the confused atomes; or some such dispersion of the simple and incorruptible Elements. . . . 'With meates and drinkes and divers charmes, they seeke to divert the chanell, that they might not die. Yet must we needs endure that blast of winde that commeth from above, though we toile and labour never so much.'

<small>Look straight forward</small>

XXVIII. He hath a stronger body, and is a better wrastler than I. What then? Is he more bountifull? is he more modest? Doth he beare all adverse chances with more equanimity: Or with his neighbours offences with more meeknesse and gentlenesse then I?

XXIX. Where the matter may be effected agreeably to that Reason, which both unto the gods, and men is common, there can be no just cause of griefe or sorrow. For where the fruit and benefit of an action well begunne and prosecuted according to the proper constitution of man may be reaped and obtained, or is sure and certaine, it is against reason that any dammage should there be suspected. In all places, and at all times, it is in thy power religiously to embrace whatsoever by Gods appointment is happened unto thee, and justly to converse with those men, whom thou hast to doe with; and accurately to examine every phancie that presents it selfe, that nothing may slippe and steale in, before thou hast rightly apprehended the true Nature of it.

XXX. Looke not about upon other mens mindes and understandings; but looke right on forwards whither Nature, both that of the Universe, in those things that happen unto thee; and thine in particular, in those things that are done by thee, doth leade, and direct thee. Now

every one is bound to doe that, which is conse- **Three**
quent and agreeable to that end which by his **chief**
true naturall constitution hee was ordained unto. **aims of a**
As for all other things, they are ordained for **able man**
the use of reasonable creatures: as in all things
wee see that that which is worse and inferiour,
is made for that which is better. Reasonable
creatures, they are ordained one for another.
That therefore which is chiefe in every mans
constitution, is, that he intend the common good.
The second is, that he yeeld not to any lusts
and motions of the flesh. For it is the part and
priviledge of the reasonable and intellective
faculty, that she can so bound her selfe, as that
neither the sensitive, nor the appetitive faculties,
may not any wayes prevaile upon her. For both
these are brutish. And therefore over both she
challengeth masterie, and cannot any waies in-
dure, if in her right temper, to be subject unto
either. And this indeed most justly. For by
nature shee was ordained to command all in the
body. The third thing proper to man by his
constitution, is, to avoid all rashnesse, and precipi-
tancie; and not to be subject to error. To these
things then, let the mind apply her selfe and goe
straight on, without any distraction about other
things, and shee hath her end, and by consequent
her happinesse.

XXXI. As one who had lived, and were
now to die by right, whatsoever is yet remaining, bestow that wholly as a gracious overplus
upon a vertuous life. Love and affect that only,
whatsoever it be that happeneth, and is by the

Within is the fountain of all good Fates appointed unto thee. For what can be more reasonable? And as any thing doth happen unto thee by way of crosse, or calamity, call to mind presently and set before thine eyes, the examples of some other men, to whom the selfe same thing did once happen likewise. Well, what did they? They grieved; they wondred; they complained. And where are they now? All dead and gone. Wilt thou also be like one of them? Or rather leaving to men of the world (whose life both in regard of themselves, and them that they converse with, is nothing but meere mutability; or men of as fickle minds, as fickle bodies; ever changing and soone changed themselves: let it be thine onely care and study, how to make a right use of all such accidents. For there is good use to be made of them, and they will prove fit matter for thee to worke upon, if it shall bee both thy care and thy desire, that whatsoever thou doest, thou thy selfe mayst like and approve thy selfe for it. And both these, see, that thou remember well, according as the diversity of the matter of the action that thou art about, shall require. Looke within; within is the fountaine of all good. Such a fountaine, where springing waters can never faile, so thou digge still deeper and deeper.

XXXII. Thou must use thy selfe also to keepe thy body fixed and steady; free from all loose fluctuant, either motion, or posture. And as upon thy face and lookes, thy minde hath easily power over them to keepe them to that which is grave

and decent; so let it challenge the same power
over the whole body also. But so observe all
things in this kinde, as that it be without any
manner of affectation.

Life like a wrestling bout

XXXIII. The art of true living in this world, is more like a wrastlers, then a dancers practise. For in this they both agree, to teach a man whatsoever falls upon him, that he may be ready for it, and that nothing may cast him downe.

XXXIV. Thou must continually ponder and consider with thy selfe, what manner of men they be, and for their mindes and understandings what is their present estate, whose good word and testimonie thou doest desire. For then neither wilt thou see cause to complaine of them that offend against their wills; or finde any want of their applause, if once thou doest but penetrate into the true force and ground both of their opinions, and of their desires. 'No soule (saith he) is willingly bereaved of the Truth,' and by consequent, neither of justice, or temperance, or kindnesse, and mildnesse; nor of any thing that is of the same kinde. It is most needfull that thou shouldest alwayes remember this. For so shalt thou be farre more gentle and moderate towards all men.

XXXV. What paine soever thou art in, let this presently come to thy minde, that it is not a thing whereof thou needest to be ashamed, neither is it a thing whereby thy understanding, that hath the government of all, can be made worse. For neither in regard of the substance of it, nor in regard of the end of it (which is, to intend the

Let not pain give thee the foil common good) can it alter and corrupt it. This also of Epicurus maist thou in most paines finde some helpe of, that it is 'neither intolerable, nor eternall;' so thou keepe thy selfe to the true bounds and limits of reason and give not way to opinion. This also thou must consider, that many things there be, which oftentimes unsensibly trouble and vexe thee, as not armed against them with patience, because they goe not ordinarily under the name of paines, which in very deed are of the same nature as paine; as to slumber unquietly, to suffer heat, to want appetite: when therefore any of these things make thee discontented, check thy selfe with these words. Now hath paine given thee the foile. Thy courage hath failed thee.

XXXVI. Take heed least at any time thou stand so affected, though towards unnaturall evill men, as ordinary men are commonly one towards another.

XXXVII. How know we whether Socrates were so Eminent indeed, and of so extraordinary a disposition? For that he dyed more gloriously, that hee disputed with the Sophists more subtilly; that hee watched in the Pagus more assiduously; that being commanded to fetch innocent Salaminius, hee refused to doe it more generously; all this will not serve. Nor that he walked in the streets, with much gravitie and majestie, as was objected unto him by his adversaries: which neverthelesse a man may well doubt of, whether it were so or no, or, which above all the rest, if so be that it were true, a man would well consider of, whether commendable, or discommendable. **What manner of soul has a man?** The thing therefore that we must inquire into, is this; what manner of soule Socrates had: whether his disposition was such; as that all that he stood upon, and sought after in this world, was barely this, That he might ever carry himselfe justly towards men, and holily towards the gods. Neither vexing himself to no purpose at the wickednesse of others, nor yet ever condescending to any mans evill fact, or evill intentions, through either feare, or ingagement of friendship. Whether of those things that happened unto him by Gods appointment, he neither did wonder at any when it did happen, or thought it intolerable in the triall of it. And lastly, whether he never did suffer his minde to sympathize with the senses, and affections of the body. For we must not think that Nature hath so mixed and tempered it with the body, as that she hath not power to circumscribe her selfe, and by her selfe to intend her owne ends and occasions.

XXXVIII. For it is a thing very possible, that a man should be a very divine man, and yet bee altogether unknowne. This thou must ever be mindfull of, as of this also, that a mans true happinesse doth consist in very few things. And that although thou doest despaire, that thou shalt ever be a good either Logician, or Naturalist, yet thou art never the further off by it from being either liberall, or modest, or charitable, or obedient unto God.

XXXIX. Free from all compulsion in all

Spend each day as though thy last cheerefulnesse and alacritie thou maist runne out thy time, though men should exclame against thee never so much, and the wilde beasts should pull in sunder the poore members of thy pampered masse of flesh. For what in either of these or the like cases, should hinder the minde to retaine her owne rest and tranquillitie, consisting both in the right judgement of those things that happen unto her, and in the ready use of all present matters and occasions? So that her judgement may say, to that which is befalne her by way of crosse: This thou art in very deed, and according to thy true nature: notwithstanding that in the judgement of opinion thou doest appeare otherwise: and her Discretion to the present object; Thou art that, which I sought for. For whatsoever it be, that is now present, shall ever be embraced by me as a fit and seasonable object, both for my reasonable faculty, and for my sociable, or charitable inclination to worke upon. And that which is principall in this matter, is that it may bee referred either unto the praise of God, or to the good of men. For either unto God or man, whatsoever it is that doth happen in the world hath in the ordinary course of nature its proper reference; neither is there any thing, that in regard of nature is either new, or reluctant and intractable, but all things both usuall and easie.

XL. Then hath a man attained to the estate of perfection in his life and conversation, when hee **so spends** every day, as if it were his last day: never hot and vehement in his affections, nor yet so cold and stupid as one that had no sense; and free from all manner of dissimulation.

Take out the beam from thine own eye

XLI. Can the gods, who are immortall, for the continuance of so many ages beare without indignation with such and so many sinners, as have ever beene, yea not only so, but also take such care for them, that they want nothing; and doest thou so grievously take on, as one that could beare with them no longer; thou that art but for a moment of time? yea thou that art one of those sinners thy selfe? A very ridiculous thing it is, that any man should dispense with vice and wickednes in himself, which is in his power to restraine; and should goe about to suppresse it in others, which is altogether impossible.

XLII. What object soever, our reasonable and sociable faculty doth meet with, that affords nothing either for the satisfaction of reason, or for the practise of charity, shee worthily doth thinke unworthy of her selfe.

XLIII. When thou hast done well, and another is benefited by thy action, must thou like a very foole looke for a third thing besides, as that it may appeare unto others also that thou hast done well, or that thou maiest in time, receive one good turne for another? No man useth to be wearie of that which is beneficiall unto him. But every action according to Nature, is beneficiall. Bee not wearie then of doing that which is beneficiall unto thee, whilest it is so unto others.

XLIV. The nature of the Universe did

> Take no thought for thy fame

once certainely before it was created, whatsoever it hath done since, deliberate and so resolve upon the creation of the World. Now since that time, whatsoever it is, that is and happens in the world, is either but a consequent of that one and first deliberation: or if so be that this ruling rationall part of the world, takes any thought and care of things particular, they are surely his reasonable and principal creatures, that are the proper object of his particular care and providence. This often thought upon, will much conduce to thy tranquillity.

The Eighth Booke

THIS also, among other things; may serve to keepe thee from vaine glory, if thou shalt consider, that thou art now altogether incapable of the commendation of one, who all his life long, or from his youth at least, hath lived a Philosophers life. For both unto others, and to thy selfe especially, it is well knowne, that thou hast done many things contrary to that perfection of life. Thou hast therefore beene confounded in thy course, and henceforth it will be hard for thee to recover the Title, and credit of a Philosopher. And to it also is thy calling and profession repugnant. If therefore thou doest truly understand, what it is that is of moment indeed; as for thy fame and credit, take no thought or care for that: let it suffice thee if all the rest of thy life, be it more or lesse, thou shalt live as thy nature requireth, or according to the true and naturall end of thy making. Take paines therefore to know what it is that thy nature requireth, and let nothing else distract thee. Thou hast already had sufficient experience, that of those many things that hitherto thou hast erred and wandred about, thou couldest not finde happinesse in any of them. Not in Syllogismes, and Logical subtilities, not in wealth, not in honour and reputation, not in pleasure. In none of all these. Wherein then is it to be found? In the practise of those things, which the nature of man, as he is a man, doth require. How then shall he doe those things? If his Dogmata, or morall Tenets and opinions (from which all motions and actions doe proceed), be right and true. Which be those Dogmata? Those that concerne that which is good or evill, as that there is nothing truly good and beneficiall unto man, but that which makes him just, temperate, courageous, liberall; and that there is nothing truly evill and hurtfull unto man, but that which causeth the contrary effects.

Wherein is happiness found?

II. Upon every action that thou art about, put this question to thy selfe; How will this when it is done agree with me? Shall I have no occasion to repent of it? Yet a very little while and I am dead and gone; and all things are at end. What then doe I care for more then this, that my present action whatsoever it be, may be the proper action of one that is

Fret not thyself because of evil-doers reasonable; whose end is, the common good; who in all things is ruled and governed by the same law of right and reason, by which God himselfe **is**.

III. Alexander, Caius, Pompeius; what are these to Diogenes, Heraclitus, and Socrates? These penetrated into the true nature of things: into all causes, and all subjects: and upon these did they exercise their power and authoritie. But as for those, as the extent of their error was, so farre did their slavery extend.

IV. What they have done, they will still doe, although thou shouldest hang thy selfe. First; Let it not trouble thee. For all things both good and evill: come to passe according to the nature and generall condition of the Universe, and within a very little while, all things will be at an end; no man will be remembred: as now of Africanus (for example) and Augustus it is already come to passe. Then secondly; Fixe thy minde upon the thing it selfe; looke into it, and remembring thy selfe, that thou art bound neverthelesse to be a good man, and what it is that thy Nature requireth of thee as thou art a man, be **not** diverted from what thou art about, and speake **that** which seemeth unto thee most just: onely speake it kindly, modestly, and without hypocrisie.

V. That which the Nature of the Universe **doth** busie her selfe about, is; that which is here, to transferre it thither, to change it, and thence againe to take it away, and to carry it to another place. So that thou needest not feare any new thing. For all things are usuall and ordinary; and all things are disposed by equality.

VI. Every particular nature hath content, when in its owne proper course it speeds. A reasonable nature doth then speed, when first in matter of phancies and imaginations, it gives no consent to that which is either false or incertaine. Secondly, when in all its motions and resolutions it takes its levell at the common good only, and that it desireth nothing, and flyeth from nothing, but what is in its owne power to compasse or avoid. And lastly, when it willingly and gladly embraceth, whatsoever is dealt and appointed unto it by the common Nature. For it is part of it; even as the nature of any one leafe, is part of the common nature of all plants and trees. But that the nature of a leafe, is part of a nature both unreasonable and unsensible, and which in its proper end may be hindered; or, which is servile and slavish: whereas the nature of man is part of a common nature which cannot be hindered, and which is both reasonable and just. From whence also it is, that according to the worth of every thing, she doth make such equall distribution of all things, as of duration, substance, forme, operation, and of events and accidents. But herein consider not whether thou shalt finde this equality in every thing absolutely and by it selfe; but whether in all the particulars of some one thing taken together, and compared with all the particulars

The proper course for a reasonable nature

Repent- of some other thing; and them together like-
ance wise.

VII. Thou hast no time nor opportunity to read. What then? Hast thou not time and opportunity to exercise thy selfe, not to wrong thy selfe; to strive against all carnall pleasures and paines, and to get the upper hand of them; to contemne honour and vaine glory; and not only, not to be angry with them, whom towards thee thou doest finde unsensible and unthankfull; but also to have a care of them still, and of their welfare?

VIII. Forbeare henceforth to complaine of the troubles of a Courtly life, either in publicke before others, or in private by thy selfe.

IX. Repentance, is an inward and selfe-reprehension for the neglect or omission of somewhat that was profitable. Now whatsoever is good, is also profitable, and it is the part of an honest vertuous man to set by it, and to make reckoning of it accordingly. But never did any honest vertuous man repent of the neglect or omission of any carnall pleasure: no carnall pleasure then is either good or profitable.

X. This, what is it in it selfe, and by it selfe, according to its proper constitution? What is the substance of it? What is the matter, or proper use? What is the forme or efficient cause? What is it for in this world, and how long will it abide? Thus must thou examine all things, that present themselves unto thee.

XI. When thou art hard to be stirred up and

awaked out of thy sleepe, admonish thy selfe and call to minde, that, to performe actions tending to the common good is that which thine owne proper constitution, and that which the nature of man doe require. But to sleepe, is common to unreasonable creatures also. And what more proper and natural, yea what more kinde and pleasing, then that which is according to Nature?

Do men gather figs of thistles?

XII. As every phancie and imagination presents it selfe unto thee, consider (if it be possible) the true nature, and the proper qualities of it, and reason with thy selfe about it.

XIII. At thy first encounter with any one, say presently to thy selfe; This man, what are his opinions concerning that which is good or evill? as concerning paine, pleasure, and the causes of both; concerning honour, and dishonour, concerning life and death; thus and thus. Now if it be no wonder that a man should have such and such opinions, how can it be a wonder that he should do such and such things? I will remember then, that he cannot but do as hee doth holding those opinions that he doth. Remember, that as it is a shame for any man to wonder that a figge tree should beare figs, so also to wonder that the World should beare any thing, whatsoever it is which in the ordinary course of nature it may beare. To a physitian also and to a pilot it is a shame either for the one to wonder, that such and such a one should have an ague; or for the other, that the winds should prove contrarie.

Complain not of what cannot be amended

XIV. Remember, that to change thy minde upon occasion, and to follow him that is able to rectifie thee, is equally ingenuous, as to finde out at the first, what is right and just, without helpe. For of thee nothing is required, that is beyond the extent of thine owne deliberation and judgement, and of thine owne understanding.

XV. If it were thine act and in thine owne power, why wouldest thou doe it? If it were not, whom doest thou accuse? the atomes, or the gods? For to doe either, is the part of a mad man. Thou must therefore blame no body, but if it be in thy power, redresse what is amisse, if it be not, to what end is it to complaine? For nothing should be done but to some certaine end.

XVI. Whatsoever dyeth and falleth, however and wheresoever it die and fall, it cannot fall out of the world. If here it have its abode and change, here also shall it have its dissolution into its proper elements. The same are the worlds Elements, and the elements of which thou doest consist. And they when they are changed, they murmur not; why shouldest thou?

XVII. Whatsoever is, was made for something: as a horse, a vine. Why wondrest thou? The Sun it selfe will say of it selfe, I was made for something; and so hath every god its proper function. What then wert thou made for? to disport and delight thy selfe? See how even common sense and reason cannot brooke it.

XVIII. Nature hath its end as well in the end and finall consummation of any thing that is, as in the beginning and continuation of it. *What is life at its basest?*

XIX. As one that tosseth up a ball. And what is a ball the better, if the motion of it be upwards; or the worse if it be downewards; or if it chance to fall upon the ground? So for the bubble; if it continue, what is it the better? and if it dissolve, what is it the worse? And so is it of a candle too. And so must thou reason with thy selfe, both in matter of fame, and in matter of death. For as for the body it selfe, (the subject of death) wouldest thou know the vilenesse of it? Turne it about, that thou maiest behold it the worst sides upwards as well, as in its more ordinarie pleasant shape; how doth it looke, when it is old and withered? when sick and pained? when in the act of lust, and fornication? And as for fame. This life is short. Both he that praiseth, and he that is praised; he that remembers, and he that is remembred, will soone be dust and ashes. Besides, it is but in one corner of this part of the world that thou art praised; and yet in this corner, thou hast not the joynt praises of all men; no nor scarce of any one constantly. And yet the whole earth it selfe, what is it but as one point, in regard of the whole world?

XX. That which must be the subject of thy consideration, is either the matter it selfe, or the Dogma, or the operation, or the true sense and signification.

XXI. Most justly have these things happened unto thee: why dost not thou amend? O but thou hadst rather become good to morrow, then to be so to day.

The course of the world

XXII. Shall I doe it? I will; so the end of my action be to doe good unto men. Doth any thing by way of crosse, or adversity happen unto me? I accept it, with reference unto the Gods, and their providence; the fountaine of all things, from which whatsoever comes to passe, doth hang and depend.

XXIII. By one action judge of the rest: This bathing which usually takes up so much of our time what is it? Oyle, sweat, filth; or the sordes of the body: an excrementitious viscositie, the excrements of oyle, and other oyntments used about the body, and mixed with the sordes of the body: all base and loathsome. And such almost is every part of our life; and every worldly object.

XXIV. Lucilla buried Verus; then was Lucilla herselfe buried by others. So Secunda Maximus, then Secunda her selfe. So Epitynchanus, Diotimus; then Epitynchanus himselfe. So Antoninus Pius, Faustina his wife; then Antoninus himselfe. This is the course of the world. First, Celer, Adrianus; then Adrianus himselfe. And those austere ones; those that foretold other mens deathes; those that were so proud and stately, where are they now? Those austere ones I meane, such as were Charax, and Demetrius, the Platonick, and Eudæmon, and others like unto those. They were all but for one day; all dead and gone long since. Some of them no sooner dead, then forgotten. Others soone turned into fables. Of others, even that which was fabulous, is now long since forgotten. This therefore thou must remember, that whatsoever thou art compounded of, shall soone be dispersed, and that thy life and breath, or thy soule: shall either be no more, or shall be translated, and appointed to some certaine place and station.

The true joy of a man

XXV. The true joy of a man, is to doe that, which properly belongs unto a man. That which is most proper unto a man, is First, to be kindly affected towards them, that are of the same kinde and nature as he is himselfe; to contemne all sensuall motions and appetites; to discerne rightly all plausible phancies and imaginations, to contemplate the nature of the Universe; both it, and all things that are done in it. In which kinde of contemplation three severall relations are to be observed. The first, to the appearant secundarie cause. The second, to the first originall cause, God, from whom originally proceeds whatsoever doth happen in the world. The third and last, to them that we live and converse with: what use may bee made of it, to their use and benefit.

XXVI. If pain be an evill, either it is in regard of the body; (and that cannot be, because the body of it selfe is altogether insensible:) or in regard of the soule. But it is in the power of the soule, to preserve her owne peace and tranquillitie, and not to suppose that paine is evill. For all judgement and deliberation; all prosecution, or aversation is

Death no respecter of persons from within, whither the sense of evill (except it bee let in by opinion) cannot penetrate.

XXVII. Wipe off all idle phancies, and say unto thy selfe incessantly; Now if I will it is in my power to keep out of this my soule all wickednesse, all lust, and concupiscences, all trouble and confusion. But on the contrary, to behold and consider all things according to their true nature, and to carry my selfe towards every thing according to its true worth. Remember then this thy power, that Nature hath given thee.

XXVIII. Whether thou speake in the Senate, or whether thou speake to any particular, let thy speech be alwayes grave and modest. But thou must not openly and vulgarly observe that sound and exact forme of speaking, concerning that which is truly good and truly evill; the vanity of the world, and of worldly men: which otherwise Truth, and Reason doth prescribe.

XXIX. Augustus his Court; His wife, his daughter, his nephewes, his sonnes in Law; his sister, Agrippa, his Kinsmen, his domestiks, his friends; Areus, Mæcenas, his aruspices or slayers of beasts for sacrifice and divination: There thou hast the death of a whole Court together. Proceed now on to the rest that have beene since that of Augustus. Hath death dealt with them otherwise, though so many and so stately whilest they lived, then it doth use to deale with any one particular man? Consider now the death of a whole kindred and familie, as of that of the Pompeyes, as that also that useth to bee written upon some monuments,

HEE WAS THE LAST OF HIS OWNE KINDRED. O what care did his predecessors take, that they might leave a successor, yet behold! at last one or other must of necessitie be THE LAST. Here again therefore consider the death of a whole kindred.

Do thy best and leave the rest

XXX. Contract thy whole life to the measure and proportion of one single action. And if in every particular action thou doest perform what is fitting to the utmost of thy power, let it suffice thee. And who can hinder thee, but that thou mayest performe what is fitting? But there may bee some outward lett and impediment. Not any, that can hinder thee, but that whatsoever thou doest, thou may doe it, justly, temperatly, and with the praise of God. Yea but there may be somewhat, whereby some operation or other of thine may be hindred. And then, with that very thing that doth hinder, thou mayest be well pleased, and so by this gentle and æquanimous conversion of thy minde unto that which may be, in stead of that which at first thou didst intend, in the roome of that former action there succeedeth another, which agrees as well with this contraction of thy life, that we now speake of.

XXXI. Receive temporall blessings without ostentation, when they are sent; and thou shalt be able to part with them with all readinesse and facility when they are taken from thee againe.

XXXII. If ever thou sawest either a hand,

Excom- or a foot, or a head lying by it selfe, in some
municate place or other, as cut off from the rest of the
from body, such must thou conceive him to make
Nature himselfe, as much as in him lyeth, that either is
offended with any thing that is happened, (whatsoever it be) and as it were divides himselfe from
it: or that commits any thing against the naturall
Law of mutuall correspondence, and society
among men: or, hee that commits any act of
uncharitablenesse. Whosoever thou art, that art
such, thou art cast forth I know not whither out
of the generall unity, which is according to
Nature. Thou wert borne indeed a part, but
now thou hast cut thy selfe off. However,
herein is matter of joy and exultation, that thou
mayst be united againe. God hath not granted
it unto any other part, that once separated and
cut off, it might be reunited, and come together
againe. But, behold, that GOODNESSE
how great and immense it is! which hath so
much esteemed MAN. As at first hee was so
made, that hee needed not, except hee would
himselfe, have divided himselfe from the whole;
so once divided and cut off, IT hath so provided
and ordered it, that if he would himselfe, hee
might returne, and grow together againe, and be
admitted into its former ranke and place of a
part, as hee was before.

XXXIII. As almost all her other faculties
and properties the nature of the Universe hath
imparted unto every reasonable Creature, so this
in particular we have received from her, that as
whatsoever doth oppose it selfe unto her, and

doth withstand her in her purposes and intentions, **How to** she doth, though against its will and intention, **keep a** bring it about to her selfe, to serve her selfe of **quiet** it in the execution of her owne destinated ends; **mind** and so by this though not intended co-operation of it with her selfe makes it part of her selfe whether it will or no. So may every reasonable Creature, what crosses or impediments soever it meets with in the course of this mortall life, it may use them as fit and proper objects, to the furtherance of whatsoever it intended, and absolutely proposed unto it selfe as its naturall end and happinesse.

XXXIV. Let not the generall representation unto thy selfe of the wretchednesse of this our mortall life, trouble thee. Let not thy minde wander up and downe, and heape together in her thoughts, the many troubles and grievous calamities which thou art as subject unto as any other. But as every thing in particular doth happen, put this question unto thy selfe, and say; What is it that in this present matter, seemes unto thee so intolerable? For thou wilt be ashamed to confesse it. Then upon this presently call to minde, that neither that which is future, nor that which is past can hurt thee; but that onely which is present. (And that also is much lessened, if thou doest rightly circumscribe it:) and then check thy minde if for so little a while, (a meere instant) it cannot hold out with patience.

XXXV. What? are either Panthea or Pergamus abiding to this day by their Masters tombes? or either Chabrias or Diotimus by that

Who is thy self? of Adrianus? O foolery! For what if they did, would their Masters be sensible of it? or if sensible, would they be glad of it? or if glad, were these immortall? Was not it appointed unto them also (both men and women,) to become old in time, and then to dye? And these once dead, what would become of these former? And when all is done, what is all this for, but for a mere bagge of blood and corruption?

XXXVI. If thou beest quick-sighted, be so in matter of judgement, and best discretion, saith he.

XXXVII. In the whole constitution of man, I see not any vertue contrary to justice, whereby it may be resisted and opposed. But one whereby pleasure and voluptuousnesse may be resisted and opposed, I see, Continence.

XXXVIII. If thou canst but withdraw conceit and opinion concerning that which may seeme hurtfull and offensive, thou thy selfe art as safe, as safe may be. Thou thy selfe? and who is that? Thy Reason. Yea, but I am not Reason. Well, be it so. How ever, let not thy Reason or understanding admit of griefe, and if there be any thing in thee that is greeved, let that, (whatsoever it be,) conceive its owne griefe, if it can.

XXXIX. That which is a hinderance of the senses, is an evill to the sensitive nature. That which is an hinderance of the appetitive and prosecutive faculty, is an evill to the sensitive nature. As of the sensitive, so of the vegetative constitution, whatsoever is an hinderance unto it, is also in that respect an evill unto the same. Why should I vex myself? And so likewise, whatsoever is an hinderance unto the minde and understanding, must needs be the proper evill of the reasonable nature. Now apply all those things unto thy selfe. Doe either paine or pleasure seize on thee? Let the senses look to that. Hast thou met with some obstacle or other in thy purpose, and intention? If thou didst propose without due reservation and exception, now hath thy reasonable part received a blow indeede. But if in generall thou didst propose unto thy selfe whatsoever might be, thou art not thereby either hurt, nor properly hindered. For in those things that properly belong unto the mind, shee cannot be hindered by any man. It is not fire, nor iron; nor the power of a tyran, nor the power of a slandering tongue; nor any thing else that can penetrate into her.

XL. If once round and solid, there is no feare that ever it will change.

XLI. Why should I grieve my selfe; who never did willingly grieve any other! One thing rejoyceth one, and another thing another. As for me, this is my joy; if my understanding be right and sound, as neither averse from any man, nor refusing any of those things, which as a man I am subject unto; If I can looke upon all things in the world meekely and kindly; accept all things, and carry my selfe towards every thing according to the true worth of the thing it selfe.

XLII. This time that is now present, bestow thou upon thy selfe. They that rather hunt for

Why should grief touch thee? fame after death, doe not consider, that those men that shall be hereafter, will be even such, as these whom now they can so hardly beare with. And besides they also will be mortall men. But to consider the thing in it selfe, if so many with so many voices, shall make such and such a sound, or shall have such and such an opinion concerning thee, what is it to thee?

XLIII. Take me and throw me where thou wilt: I am indifferent. For there also I shall have that Spirit which is within me propitious; that is well pleased and fully contented both in that constant disposition, and with those particular actions, which to its owne proper constitution are sutable and agreeable.

XLIV. Is this then a thing of that worth, that for it my soule should suffer, and become worse then it was? as either basely dejected, or disordinately affected, or confounded within it selfe, or terrified? What can there be, that thou shouldest so much esteeme?

XLV. Nothing can happen unto thee, which is not incidentall unto thee, as thou art a man. As nothing can happen either to an oxe, a vine, or to a stone, which is not incidentall unto them; unto every one in his owne kinde. If therefore nothing can happen unto any thing, which is not both usuall and naturall; why art thou displeased? Sure the common nature of all would not bring any thing upon any, that were intolerable. If therefore it be a thing externall that causeth thy griefe, know, that it is not that properly that doth cause it, but thine owne conceit and opinion concerning the thing: which thou mayest rid thy selfe of, when thou wilt. But if it be somewhat that is amisse in thine owne disposition, that doth grieve thee, mayest thou not rectifie thy moral Tenets and opinions. But if it grieve thee, that thou doest not performe that which seemeth unto thee right and just, why doest not thou choose rather to performe it then to grieve? But somewhat that is stronger then thy selfe doth hinder thee. Let it not grieve thee then, if it be not thy fault that the thing is not performed. Yea but it is a thing of that nature, as that thy life is not worth the while, except it may be performed. If it be so, upon condition that thou be kindly and lovingly disposed towards all men, thou mayest be gone. For even then, as much as at any time, art thou in a very good estate of performance, when thou doest die in charity with those, that are an obstacle unto thy performance.

Grief and Reason

XLVI. Remember that thy minde is of that nature as that it becommeth altogether unconquerable, when once recollected in her selfe, shee seekes no other content then this, that she cannot be forced: yea though it so fall out, that it be even against Reason it selfe, that it doth bandie. How much lesse when by the help of Reason she is able to judge of things with discretion? And therefore let thy chiefe fort and place of defence be, a minde free from passions. A stronger place, (whereunto to make his refuge, and so to become impregnable) and better fortified then this, hath no man. He that seeth not

Shavings in Nature's workshop this is unlearned. Hee that seeth it, and betaketh not himselfe to this place of refuge; is unhappy.

XLVII. Keepe thyselfe to the first bare and naked apprehensions of things, as they present themselves unto thee, and adde not unto them. It is reported unto thee, that such a one speaketh ill of thee. Well; that he speaketh ill of thee, so much is reported. But that thou art hurt thereby, is not reported: That is the addition of opinion, which thou must exclude. I see that my child is sick. That hee is sick, I see, but that he is in danger of his life also, I see it not. Thus thou must use to keepe thy selfe to the first motions and apprehensions of things, as they present themselves outwardly; and adde not unto them from within thy selfe through meere conceit and opinion. Or rather adde unto them; but as one that understandeth the true nature of all things that happen in the world.

XLVIII. Is the cucumber bitter? **set it** away. Brambles are in the way? avoid them. Let this suffice. Adde not presently speaking unto thy selfe, What serve these things for in the world? For, this, one that is acquainted with the mysteries of Nature, will laugh at thee for it; as a Carpenter would or a Shoo-maker, if meeting in either of their shops with some shavings, or small remnants of their worke, thou shouldest blame them for it. And yet those men, it is not for want of a place where to throw them that they keepe them in their shops for a while: but the nature of the Universe hath no such out-place:

but herein **doth** consist the wonder of her art and skill, that shee having once circumscribed her selfe within some certain bounds and limits, whatsoever is within her that seemes either corrupted, or old, or unprofitable, she can change it into her selfe, and of these very things can make new things; so that shee needeth not to seeke elsewhere out of her selfe either for a new supply of matter and substance, or for a place where to throw out whatsoever is irrecoverably putrid and corrupt. Thus shee, as for place, so for matter and art, is her selfe sufficient unto her selfe. *Nature a marvellous artist*

XLIX. Not to be slack and negligent; **or** loose, and wanton in thy actions, nor contentious, and troublesome in thy conversation, nor to rove and wander in thy phancies and imaginations. Not basely to contract thy soule; nor boistrously to sally out with it, or, furiously to launch out as it were, nor ever to want employment.

L. They kill me, they cut my flesh: they persecute my person with curses. What then? May not thy minde for all this continue pure, prudent, temperate, just? As a fountaine of sweet and cleere water, though she be cursed by some stander by, yet do her springs neverthelesse still runne as sweet and cleere as before; yea though either durt or dung be throwne in, yet is it no sooner throwne, then dispersed, and she cleared. Shee cannot be dyed or, infected by it. What then must I doe, that I may have within **my** selfe an overflowing fountaine, and not a well? Beget thy selfe by continuall paines and

^{Whose} endeavours to true liberty with charity, and true
^{praise} simplicity and modesty.
^{is worth}
^{having?} LI. He that knoweth not what the world is, knoweth not where he himself is. And he that knoweth not what the world was made for, cannot possibly know either what are the qualities, or what is the nature of the world. Now he that in either of these is to seeke, for what he himselfe was made, is ignorant also. What then dost thou thinke of that man, who proposeth unto himselfe, as a matter of great moment, the noyse and applause of men, who both where they are, and what they are themselves, are altogether ignorant? Dost thou desire to be commended of that man, who thrice in one houre perchance, doth himselfe curse himselfe? Doest thou desire to please him, who pleaseth not himselfe? or doest thou thinke that hee pleaseth himselfe, who doth use to repent himselfe almost of every thing that he doth?

LII. Not only now henceforth to have a common breath, or to hold correspondencie of breath, with that Ayre, that compasseth us about; but to have a common minde, or to hold correspondencie of minde also with that rationall substance, which compasseth all things. For, that also is of it selfe, and of its own nature (if a man can but draw it in as he should) every where diffused; and passeth through all things, no lesse then the Ayre doth, if a man can but suck it in.

LIII. Wickednesse in generall doth not hurt the World. Particular wickednesse doth not hurt any other: onely unto **him it** is hurtfull, whosoever he be that offends, **unto** whom in great favour and mercie it is granted, that whensoever he himselfe shall but first desire it, he may be presently delivered of it. Unto my Free-will my neighbours free-will, who ever he be, (as his life, or his body), is altogether indifferent. For though we are all made one for another, yet have our minds and understandings, each of them their owne proper and limited jurisdiction. For else another mans wickednesse might be my evill; which God would not have, that it might not be in another mans power to make me unhappy: which nothing now can doe but mine owne wickednesse.

Wrong hurts none but the doer

LIV. The Sun seemeth to be shed abroad. And indeed it is diffused but not effused. For that diffusion of it is a τάσις or an extension. For therefore are the beams of it called ἀκτῖνες from the word ἐκτείνεσθαι, to be stretched out and extended. Now what a Sun beame is, thou mayest know if thou observe the light of the Sun, when through some narrow hole it pierceth into some roome that is dark. For it is alwayes in a direct line. And as by any solid body, that it meetes with in the way that is not penetrable by ayre, it is divided and abrupted, and yet neither slides off, or falls downe, but stayeth there neverthelesse: such must the diffusion of the minde be; not an effusion, but an extension. What obstacles and impediments soever shee meeteth with in her way, shee must not violently, and by way of an impetuous onset

Either light upon them; neither must shee fall downe;
no evil but she must stand, and give light unto that
or which doth admit of it. For as for that which
another
life doth not, it is its owne fault and losse, if it bereave it selfe of her light.

LV. He that feareth Death, either feareth that he shall have no sense at all, or that his senses will not be the same. Whereas, he should rather comfort himselfe, that either no sense at all, and so no sense of evill; or if any sense, then another life, and so no death properly.

LVI. All men are made one for another: either then teach them better, or beare with them.

LVII. The motion of the mind, is not as the motion of a dart. For the minde when it is wary and cautelous, and by way of diligent circumspection turneth her selfe many wayes, may then as well be said to goe straight on to the object, as when it useth no such circumspection.

LVIII. To pierce and penetrate into the estate of every ones understanding that thou hast to do with: as also to make the estate of thine owne open, and penetrable to any other.

The Ninth Booke

HE that is unjust, is also impious. For the Nature of the Universe, having made all reasonable creatures one for another, to the end that they should do one another good; more or lesse according to the severall persons and occasions; but in no wise hurt one another: it is manifest that hee that doth transgresse against this her will, is guilty of impiety towards the most ancient and venerable of all the Deities. For the Nature of the Universe, is the nature the common Parent of all, and therefore piously to be observed of all things that are, and that which now is, to whatsoever first was, and gave it its being, hath relation of blood and kindred. Shee is also called Truth; and is the first cause of all truths. He therefore that willingly and wittingly doth lye, is impious in that he doth receive, and so commit injustice: but hee that against his will, in that he disagreeth from the nature of the Universe, and in that striving with the nature of the World he doth in his particular, violate the generall order of the world. For hee doth no better then strive and warre against it, who contrary to his owne Nature applieth himselfe to that which is contrary to truth. For Nature had before furnisht him with instincts and opportunities sufficient for the attainement of it; which he having hitherto neglected, is not now able to discerne that which is false from that which is true. Hee also that pursues after pleasures, as that which is truely good; and flies from paines, as that which is truely evill, is impious. For such a one must of necessity oftentimes accuse that common Nature, as distributing many things both unto the evill, and unto the good, not according to the deserts of

What is impiety?

Regard things as Nature does

either: as unto the bad oftentimes pleasures, and the causes of pleasures; So unto the good, paines, and the occasions of paines. Againe, he that feareth paines and crosses in this world, feareth some of those things which sometime or other must needes happen in the world. And that wee have already showed to be impious. And hee that pursueth after pleasures, will not spare, to compasse his desires to doe that which is unjust, and that is manifestly impious. Now those things which unto Nature are equally indifferent (for she had not created both, both paine and pleasure, if both had not beene unto her equally indifferent): they that will live according to Nature, must in those things (as being of the same minde and disposition that shee is) be as equally indifferent. Whosoever therefore in either matter of pleasure and paine; death and life; honour and dishonour, (which things Nature in the administration of the world, indifferently doth make use of), is not as indifferent, it is apparent that hee is impious. When I say that common Nature doth indifferently make use of them, my meaning is, that they happen indifferently in the ordinary course of things, which by a necessary consequence, whether as principall or accessorie, come to passe in the world, according to that first and ancient deliberation of Providence, by which shee from some certaine beginning, did resolve upon the creation of such a World, conceiving then in her wombe as it were some certaine rational generative seedes and faculties of things future, whether subjects, changes, successions; both such and such, and just so many.

II. It were indeed more happy and comfortable, for a man to depart out of this World, having lived all his life long cleare from all falsehood, dissimulation, voluptuousnesse, and pride. But if this cannot be, yet is it some comfort for a man joyfully to depart as weary, and out of love with those; rather then to desire to live, and to continue long in those wicked courses. Hath not yet experience taught thee to flye from the plague? For a farre greater plague is the corruption of the minde, then any certaine change and distemper of the common aire can be. This is a plague of creatures, as they are living creatures; but that of men as they are men or reasonable.

III. Thou must not in matter of death, carry thy selfe scornfully, but as one that is well pleased with it, as being one of those things that Nature hath appointed. For what thou dost conceive of these, of a boy to become a young man, to waxe old, to grow, to ripen, to get teeth, or a beard, or grey haires; to beget, to beare, or to be delivered; or what other action soever it be, that is naturall unto man according to the severall seasons of his life; such a thing is it also to be dissolved. It is therefore the part of a wise man, in matter of death, not in any wise to carry himselfe either violently, or proudly; but patiently to wayte for it, as one of Natures operations: that with the same minde as now thou doest expect when that which yet is but an Embryo in thy Wifes belly shall come forth; thou mayst ex-

Wait patiently for Death

Make haste, O Death pect also when thy soule shall fall off from that outward coat or skinne : wherein as a childe in the belly it lieth involved and shut up.* But if thou desirest a more popular, and though not so direct and philosophicall, yet a very powerfull and penetrative receipt against the feare of death, Nothing can make thee more willing to part with thy life, then if thou shalt consider, both **what** the subjects themselves are that thou shalt part with, and what manner of dispositions thou shalt no more have to doe with. True it is, that offended with them thou must not be by no meanes, but take care of them, and meekely beare with them. However, this thou mayest remember, that whensoever it happens that thou depart, it shall not be from men that held the same opinions that thou doest. For that indeede, (if it were so) is the onely thing that might make thee averse from death, and willing to continue here, if it were thy hap to live with men that had obtained the same beliefe that thou hast. But now, what a toyle it is for thee to live with men of different opinions, thou seest: so that thou hast rather occasion to say, Hasten, I thee pray, O Death; least I also in time forget my selfe.

IV. He that sinneth, sinneth unto himselfe. Hee that is unjust, hurts himselfe, in that he makes himselfe worse then he was before. Not he onely that committeth, but he also that omitteth some thing, is oftentimes unjust.

V. If my present apprehension of the object be right, and my present action charitable, and this, towards whatsoever doth proceed from God, be Earth to my present disposition, to be well pleased with it, earth it sufficeth.

VI. To wipe away phancie, to use deliberation, to quench concupiscence, to keepe the minde free to her selfe.

VII. Of all unreasonable creatures, there is but one unreasonable soul; and of all that are reasonable, but one reasonable Soule, divided betwixt them all. As of all earthly things there is but one Earth, and but one light that we see by; and but one ayre that we breath in, as many as either breath or see. Now whatsoever partakes of some common thing, naturally affects and enclines unto that whereof it is part, being of one kinde and nature with it. Whatsoever is Earthly, presseth downwards to the common Earth. Whatsoever is liquid, would flow together. And whatsoever is ayrie, would be together likewise. So that without some obstacle, and some kinde of violence, they cannot well be kept asunder. Whatsoever is fiery, doth not onely by reason of the Elementarie fire tend upwards; but here also is so ready to joyne, and to burne together, that whatsoever doth want sufficient moisture to make resistance, is easily set on fire. Whatsoever therefore is partaker of that reasonable common Nature, naturally doth as much and more long after his owne kinde. For by how much in its owne nature it excells all other things, by so much more is it desirous to be joyned and united unto that, which is of its owne nature. As for unreasonable creatures then, they had not long

Nature must prevail beene, but presently begun among them swarmes, and flocks, and broods of young ones, and a kinde of mutuall love and affection. For though but unreasonable, yet a kinde of soule these had, and therefore was that naturall desire of union more strong and intense in them, as in creatures of a more excellent nature, then either in plants, or stones, or trees. But among reasonable creatures, begunne common-wealths, friendships, families, publick meetings, and even in their warres conventions and truces. Now among them that were yet of a more excellent nature, as the starres and planets, though by their nature farre distant one from another, yet even among them beganne some mutuall correspondencie and unitie. So proper is it to excellencie in a high degree to affect unitie, as that even in things so farre distant, it could operate unto a mutuall Sympathie. But now behold, what is now come to passe. Those creatures that are reasonable, are now the only creatures that have forgotten their naturall affection and inclination of one towards another. Among them alone of all other things that are of one kinde, there is not to be found a general disposition to flow together. But though they fly from Nature, yet are they stopt in their course, and apprehended. Doe they what they can, Nature doth prevaile. And so shalt thou confesse, if thou doest observe it. For sooner mayest thou finde a thing earthly, where no earthly thing is, then finde a man that naturally can live by himselfe alone.

VIII. Man, God, the World, every one in

their kinde, beare some fruits. All things have their proper time to beare. Though by custome, the word it selfe is in a manner become proper unto the vine, and the like, yet is it so neverthelesse, as wee have said. As for reason, that beareth both common fruit for the use of others; and peculiar, which it selfe doth enjoy. Reason is of a diffusive nature, what it selfe is in it selfe, it begets in others, and so doth multiply.

Trouble is within and may be cast out

IX. Either teach them better if it be in thy power; or if it be not, remember that for this use, to beare with them patiently, was mildnesse and goodnesse granted unto thee. The gods themselves are good unto such; yea and in some things, (as in matter of health, of wealth, of honour,) are content often to further their endeavours: so good and gracious are they. And mightest thou not be so too? or, tell me, what doth hinder thee?

X. Labour not as one to whom it is appointed to be wretched, nor as one that either would be pittied, or admired; but let this be thine only care and desire; so alwayes and in all things to prosecute or to forbeare, as the law of Charity, or mutuall society doth require.

XI. This day I did come out of all my trouble. Nay I have cast out all my trouble; it should rather be. For that which troubled thee, whatsoever it was, was not without any where that thou shouldest come out of it, but within in thine owne opinions, from whence it must be cast out, before thou canst truly and constantly be at ease.

XII. All those things, for matter of experience are usuall and ordinarie; for their continuance but for a day; and for their matter, most base, and filthy. As they were in the days of those whom we have buried, so are they now also, and no otherwise.

XIII. The things themselves that affect us, they stand without doores, neither knowing any thing themselves nor able to utter any thing unto others concerning themselves. What then is it, that passeth verdict on them? The understanding.

XIV. As vertue and wickednesse consist not in passion, but in action; so neither doth the true good or evill of a reasonable charitable man consist in passion, but in operation and action.

XV. To the stone that is cast up, when it comes downe it is no hurt unto it; as neither benefit, when it doth ascend.

XVI. Sift their mindes and understandings, and behold what men they be, whom thou doest stand in feare of what they shall judge of thee, what they themselves judge of themselves.

XVII. All things that are in the world, are alwayes in the estate of alteration. Thou also art in a perpetuall change, yea and under corruption too, in some part: and so is the whole world.

XVIII. It is not thine, but another mans sinne. Why should it trouble thee? Let him looke to it, whose sinne it is.

XIX. Of an operation and of a purpose there is an ending, or of an action and of a purpose we say commonly, that it is at an end: from opinion also there is an absolute cessation, which is as it

The stone that is cast up

were the death of it. In all this there is no
hurt. Apply this now to a mans age, as first, a
child; then a youth, then a young man, then an
old man; every change from one age to another
is a kinde of death. And all this while here is
no matter of griefe yet. Passe now unto that
life first, that which thou livedst under thy
Grandfather, then under thy Mother, then under
thy Father. And thus when through the whole
course of thy life hitherto thou hast found and
observed many alterations, many changes, many
kindes of endings and cessations, put this question
to thy selfe, what matter of griefe or sorrow dost
thou finde in any of these? Or what doest thou
suffer through any of these? If in none of these,
then neither in the ending and consummation of
thy whole life, which is also but a cessation and
change.

Death and Change

XX. As occasion shall require, either to thine
owne Understanding, or to that of the Universe, or
to his, whom thou hast now to doe with, let thy
refuge be with all speed. To thine owne, that it
resolve upon nothing against justice. To that of
the Universe, that thou maist remember, part of
whom thou art. Of his, that thou mayest consider, whether in the estate of ignorance, or of
knowledge. And then also must thou call to
minde, that he is thy Kinsman.

XXI. As thou thy selfe, who ever thou art,
wert made for the perfection and consummation,
being a member of it, of a common society; so
must every action of thine tend to the perfection
and consummation of a life that is truly sociable.

Life a phantom farce What action soever of thine therefore that either immediately or afarre off, hath not reference to the common good, that is an exorbitant, and disorderly action; yea it is seditious; as one among the people who from such and such a consent and unity, should factiously divide and separate himselfe.

XXII. Childrens anger, meere bables; wretched soules bearing up dead bodies, that they may not have their fall so soone: Even as it is in that common dirge song.

XXIII. Goe to the qualitie of the cause from which the effect doth proceed. Behold it by it selfe bare and naked, separated from all that is materiall. Then consider the utmost bounds of time that that cause, thus and thus qualified, can subsist and abide.

XXIV. Infinite are the troubles and miseries, that thou hast already beene put to, by reason of this only, because that for all happinesse it did not suffice thee, or, that thou didst not account it sufficient happinesse, that thy understanding did operate according to its naturall constitution.

XXV. When any shall either impeach thee with false accusations, or hatefully reproach thee, or shall use any such carriage towards thee, get thee presently to their mindes and understandings, and looke in them, and behold what manner of men they bee. Thou shalt see, that there is no such occasion why it should trouble thee, what such as they are thinke of thee. Yet must thou love them still, for by nature they are thy friends.

And the gods themselves, in those things that they seeke from them as matters of great moment, are well content, all manner of wayes, as by dreames and oracles, to helpe them as well as others.

If God is, then all is well

XXVI. Up and downe, from one age to another, goe the ordinarie things of the world; being still the same. And either of every thing in particular before it come to passe, the minde of the Universe doth consider with it selfe and deliberate: And if so, then submit for shame unto the determination of such an excellent Understanding: or once for all it did resolve upon all things in generall; and since that whatsoever happens, happens by a necessary consequence, and all things indivisibly in a manner and inseparably hold one of another. In summe, either there is a God, and then all is well; or if all things goe by chance and fortune, yet maist thou use thine owne providence in those things that concerne thee properly; and then art thou well.

XXVII. Within a while the Earth shall cover us all, and then shee her selfe shall have her change. And then the course will be, from one period of eternitie unto another, and so a perpetuall eternitie. Now can any man that shall consider with himselfe in his mind the severall rollings, or successions, of so many changes and alterations, and the swiftnesse of all these rollings; can he otherwise but contemne in his heart and despise all worldly things? The Cause of the Universe, is as it were a strong torrent, it carrieth all away.

> Do not expect too much

XXVIII. And these your professed politicians, the only true practick philosophers of the world, (as they thinke of themselves) so full of affected gravitie, or such profest lovers of vertue and honestie, what wretches be they in very deed; how vile and contemptible in themselves? O man! what a doe doest thou keepe? Doe what thy nature doth now require. Resolve upon it, if thou mayest: and take no thought, whether any body shall know it or no. Yea, but sayest thou, I must not expect a Plato's common-wealth. If they profit though never so little, I must be content; and thinke much even of that little progresse. Doth then any of them forsake their former false opinions that I should think they profit? For without a change of opinions, alas! what is all that ostentation, but meere wretchednesse of slavish mindes, that groane privately, and yet would make a shew of obedience to Reason, and Truth? Goe too now and tell me of Alexander and Philippus, and Demetrius Phalereus. Whether they understood what the common nature requireth, and could rule themselves or no, they know best themselves. But if they kept a life, and swaggered; I (God be thanked) am not bound to imitate them. The effect of true Philosophie is, unaffected simplicity and modesty. Perswade me not to ostentation and vaine glory.

XXIX. From some high place as it were to looke downe, and to behold here flocks, and there sacrifices, without number; and all kinde **The sum** of navigation; some in a ruffe and stormie sea, **of all** and some in a calme: the general differences, **philo-** or different estates of things, some, that are **sophy** now first upon being; the severall and mutuall relations of those things that are together; and some other things that are at their last. Their lives also, who were long agoe, and theirs who shall be hereafter, and the present estate and life of those many nations of Barbarians that are now in the world, thou must likewise consider in thy minde. And how many there be, who never so much as heard of thy Name, how many that will soone forget it; how many who but even now did commend thee, within a very little while perchance will speake ill of thee. So that neither fame, nor honour, nor any thing **else that** this world doth afford, is worth the while. The summe then of all; Whatsoever doth happen unto thee, whereof God is the cause, to accept it contentedly: whatsoever thou **doest,** whereof thou thyselfe art the cause; to **doe it** justly: which will be, if both in thy **resolution** and in thy action thou have no fur-**ther** end, then **to** doe good unto others, as being that, which by thy naturall constitution, as a man, thou art bound unto.

XXX. Many of those things that trouble and straighten thee, it is in thy power to cut off, as wholly depending from meere conceit and opinion, and then thou shalt have roome enough.

XXXI. To comprehend the whole world together in thy minde, and the whole course

As it was in the beginning of this present age to represent it unto thy selfe, and to fixe thy thoughts upon the suddaine change of every particular object. How short the time is from the generation of any thing, unto the dissolution of the same; but how immense and infinite both that which was before the generation, and that which after the generation of it shall be. All things that **thou** seest, will soone be perished, and they that see their corruptions, will soone vanish away themselves. Hee that dieth a hundred yeares old, and he that dieth young, shall come all to one.

XXXII. What are their mindes and understandings; and what the things that they apply themselves unto: what doe they love, and what doe they hate for? Phancie to thy selfe the estate of their soules openly to be seene. When they thinke they hurt them shrewdly, whom they speake ill of; and when they thinke they doe them a very good turne, whom they commend and extoll: O how full are they then of conceit, and opinion!

XXXIII. Losse and corruption, is **in** very deed nothing else but change and alteration; and that is it, which the Nature of the Universe doth most delight in, by which, and according to which, whatsoever is done, is well done. For that was the estate of worldly things from the beginning, and so shall it ever be. Or wouldest thou rather say, that all things in the world have gone ill from the beginning for so many Ages, and shall ever goe ill? And then among so many Deities, could no Divine power be found all this while, that could rectifie the things of the world? Cease thy murmuring Or is the world, to incessant woes and miseries, for ever condemned?

XXXIV. How base and putrid, every common matter is! Water, dust, and from the mixture of these bones, and all that loathsome stuffe that our bodies doe consist of; so subject to bee infected, and corrupted. And againe those other things that are so much prized and admired, as marble stones, what are they, but as it were the Kernels of the Earth? gold and silver, what are, but as the more grosse fæces of the Earth? Thy most royall apparel, for matter, it is but as it were the haire of a silly sheepe, and for colour, the very blood of a shell fish; of this nature are all other things. Thy life it selfe, is some such thing too; a meere exhalation of blood: and it also, apt to be changed into some other common thing.

XXXV. Will this querulousnesse, this murmuring, this complaining and dissembling never bee at an end? What then is it, that troubleth thee? Doth any new thing happen unto thee? What doest thou so wonder at? At the Cause, or the matter? Behold either by it selfe, is either of that weight and moment indeede? And besides these, there is not any thing. But thy duty towards the Gods also, it is time that thou shouldest acquit thy selfe of it with more goodnesse and simplicity.

XXXVI. It is all one to see these things for a hundred of yeares together, or but for three yeares.

XXXVII. If he have sinned, his is the harme, not mine. But perchance he hath not.

What the Gods can do

XXXVIII. Either all things by the providence of Reason happen unto every particular, as a part of one generall body; and then it is against reason that a part should complaine of any thing that happens for the good of the Whole; or if, according to Epicurus, Atoms be the Cause of all things and that life be nothing else but an accidentarie confusion of things, and death nothing else, but a meere Dispersion and so of all other things: what doest thou trouble thy selfe for?

XXXIX. Sayest thou unto that Rationall part, Thou art dead; corruption hath taken hold on thee? Doth it then also voide excrements? Doth it like either Oxen, or sheepe, graze or feede; that it also should be mortall, as well as the body?

XL. Either the Gods can doe nothing for us at all, or they can still and alay all the distractions and distempers of thy minde. If they can doe nothing, why doest thou pray? If they can, why wouldst not thou rather pray, that they will grant unto thee, that thou mayst neither feare, nor lust after any of those worldly things which cause these distractions, and distempers of it? Why not rather, that thou mayst not at either their absence or presence, bee grieved and discontented: then either that thou mayst obtaine them, or that thou maist avoyde them? For certainly it must needs be, that if the Gods can help us in any thing, they may in this kinde also. But thou wilt say perchance, In those things the Gods have given me my liberty: and it is in mine owne power to doe what I will. But if thou mayest use this liberty, rather to set thy minde at true liberty, then wilfully with basenesse and servility of minde, to affect those things, which either to compasse or to avoyde is not in thy power, wert not thou better? And as for the Gods, who hath told thee, that they may not helpe us up even in those things that they have put in our owne power? Whether it be so or no, thou shalt soone perceive, if thou wilt but try thy selfe and pray. One prayeth that he may compasse his desire, to lye with such or such a one, pray thou that thou mayest not lust to lye with her. Another how hee may be rid of such a one; pray thou that thou mayest so patiently beare with him, as that thou have no such neede to be rid of him. Another, that hee may not lose his child. Pray thou that thou mayst not feare to lose him. To this end and purpose, let all thy prayer be, and see what will be the event. *After this manner pray*

XLI. 'In my sicknesse' (sayeth Epicurus of himselfe:) 'my discourses were not concerning the nature of my disease, neither was that, to them that came to visite mee, the subject of my talke; but in the consideration and contemplation of that, which was of especiall weight and moment, was all my time bestowed and spent, and among others in this very thing, how my minde, by a naturall and unavoydable sympathie partaking in some sort with the present indis-

A stedfast mind position of my body, might netherthelesse keepe herselfe free from trouble, and in present possession of her owne proper happinesse. Neither did I leave the ordering of my body to Physicians altogether to doe with me what they would, as though I expected any great matter from them, or as though I thought it a matter of such **great** consequence, by their meanes to recover my health: for my present estate, me thought, liked me very well, and gave me good content.' Whether therefore in sicknesse (if thou chance to sicken) or in what other kinde of extremity soever, endeavour thou also to be in thy minde so affected, as hee doth report of himselfe: not to depart from thy philosophie for any thing that can befall thee, nor to give eare to the discourses of silly people, and meere naturalists.

XLII. It is common to all trades and professions to minde and intend that only, which now they are about, and the instrument whereby they worke.

XLIII. When at any time thou art offended with any ones impudencie, put presently this question to thy selfe; What? Is it then possible, that there should not be any impudent men in the world! Certainly it is not possible. Desire not then that which is impossible. For this one, (thou must thinke) whosoever he be, is one of those impudent ones, that the world cannot be without. So of the subtle and craftie, so of the perfidious, so of every one that offendeth, must thou ever be ready to reason with thy selfe. For whilest in generall thou doest thus reason with thy selfe, that the kinde of them must needs be **Nature's antidotes** in the world, thou wilt be the better able to use meeknesse towards every particular. This also thou shalt find of very good use, upon every such occasion, presently to consider with thy selfe, what proper vertue nature hath furnished man with, against such a vice, or to encounter with a disposition vicious in this kinde. As for example, against the unthankfull, it hath given goodnesse and meeknesse, as an antidote, and so against another vicious in another kinde some other peculiar facultie. And generally, is it not in thy power to instruct him better, that is in an error? For whosoever sinneth, doth in that decline from his purposed end, and is certainly deceived. And againe, what art thou the worse for his sinne? For thou shalt not find that any **one** of these, against whom thou art incensed, hath in very deed done any thing whereby thy minde (the only true subject of thy hurt and evill) can be made worse, then it was. And what a matter of either griefe or wonder is this, if he that is unlearned, doe the deeds of one that is unlearned? Should not thou rather blame **thy self, who, when** upon very good grounds **of** reason, thou mightst have thought it very probable, that such a thing would by **such a one** be committed, didst not onely not foresee it, but moreover doest wonder at it, that such a thing should be. But then especially, when thou doest finde fault with either an unthankfull, or a false man, must thou reflect upon thy selfe. For without all question, thou thy selfe art much in

Goodness its own reward fault, if either of one that were of such a disposition thou didst expect that he should be true unto thee: or when unto any thou didst a good turne, thou didst not there bound thy thoughts, as one that had obtained his end; nor didst not thinke that from the action it selfe thou hadst received a full reward of the good that thou hadst done. For what wouldst thou have more? Unto him that is a man, thou hast done a good turne: doth not that suffice thee? What thy nature required, that hast thou done. Must thou be rewarded for it? As if either the eye for that it seeth, or the feet that they goe, should require satisfaction. For as these being by nature appointed for such an use, can challenge no more, then that they may worke according to their naturall constitution: so man being borne to do good unto others whensoever he doth a reall good unto any by helping them out of errour; or though but in middle things, as in matter of wealth, life, preferment, and the like, doth helpe to further their desires; he doth that for which he was made, and therefore can require no more.

The Tenth Booke

O MY soule, the time I trust will be, when thou shalt be good, simple, single, more open and visible, then that body by which it is inclosed. Thou wilt one day be sensible of their happinesse, whose end is love, and their affections dead to all worldly things. **Thou** shalt one day be full, and in want of no externall thing: not seeking pleasure from any thing, either living or unsensible, that this World can afford; neither wanting time for the continuation of thy pleasure, nor place and opportunitie, nor the favour either of the weather or of men. When thou shalt have content in thy present estate, and all things present shall adde to thy content: when thou shalt perswade thy selfe, that thou hast all **things;** all for thy good, and all by the providence of the gods: and of things future also shalt be as confident, that all will doe well, as tending to the maintenance and preservation in some sort, of his perfect welfare and happinesse, who is perfection of life, of goodnesse, and beautie; Who begets all things, and containeth all things in himselfe, and in himselfe doth recollect all things from all places that are dissolved, that of them he may beget others againe like unto them. Such one day shall be thy disposition, that thou shalt be able, both in regard of the gods, and in regard of men, so to fit and **order** thy conversation, as neither to complaine of **them** at any time, for any thing that they doe; **nor to** doe any thing thy selfe, for which thou mayest justly be condemned.

Aspirations

II. As one who is altogether governed by nature, let it be thy care to observe what it is that thy nature in generall doth require. That done, if thou finde not that thy nature, as thou art a living sensible creature, will be the worse for it, thou mayest proceed. Next then thou must

How to bear what happens examine, what thy nature as thou art **a living** sensible creature, doth require. And that, whatsoever it be, thou mayest admit of and doe it, if thy nature as thou art a reasonable living creature, will not be the worse for it. Now whatsoever is reasonable, is also sociable. Keep thy selfe to these rules, and trouble not thy selfe about idle things.

III. Whatsoever doth happen unto thee, thou art naturally by thy naturall constitution either able, or not able to beare. If thou beest able, be not offended, but beare it according to thy naturall constitution, or as nature hath inabled thee. If thou beest not able, be not offended. For it will soone make an end of thee, and it selfe, (whatsoever it be) at the same time end with thee. But remember, that whatsoever by the strength of opinion, grounded upon a certaine apprehension of both true profit and duty, thou canst conceive tolerable; that thou art able to beare that by thy naturall constitution.

IV. Him that offends, to teach with love and meeknesse, and to shew him his error. But if thou canst not, then to blame thy selfe, or rather not thy selfe neither, if thy will **and** endeavours have not been wanting.

V. Whatsoever it be that happens unto thee, it is that which from all time was appointed unto thee. For by the same coherence of causes, by which thy substance from all eternitie was appointed to bee, was also whatsoever should happen unto it, destinated and appointed.

VI. Either with Epicurus, we must fondly

imagine the atomes to be the cause of all things, **Man a**
or wee must needs grant a Nature. Let this **part of**
then bee thy first ground, that thou art part of **Nature**
that Universe, which is governed by nature.
Then secondly, that to those parts that are of
the same kinde and Nature as thou art, thou
hast relation of kindred. For of these, if I
shall alwayes be mindfull, first as I am a part, I
shall never be displeased with any thing, that
falls to my particular share of the common
chances of the world. For nothing that is
behoovefull unto the whole, can be truly hurtfull to that which is part of it. For this being
the common priviledge of all natures, that they
containe nothing in themselves that is hurtfull
unto them ; it cannot be that the nature of the
Universe (whose priviledge beyond other particular natures, is, that shee cannot against her
will by any higher externall cause be constrained,) should beget any thing and cherish
it in her bosome that should tend to her owne
hurt and prejudice. As then I beare in minde
that I am a part of such an Universe, I shall not
be displeased with any thing that happens. And
as I have relation of kindred to those parts that
are of the same kinde and nature that I am, so I
shall be carefull to doe nothing that is prejudiciall to the communitie, but in all my delibera-
tions shall they that are of my Kinde ever be ;
and the common good, that, which all my intentions and resolutions shall drive unto, as that
which is contrary unto it, I shall by all meanes
endeavour **to** prevent and avoid. These things

Nature's changes once so fixed and concluded, as thou wouldest thinke him an happy citizen, whose constant studie and practise were for the good and benefit of his fellow Citizens, and the cariage of the Citie such towards him, that he were well pleased with it; so must it needs be with thee, that thou shalt live a happy life.

VII. All parts of the world, (all things I meane that are contained within the whole world,) must of necessity at some time or other come to corruption. Alteration I should say, to speake truly and properly; but that I may be the better understood, I am content at this time to use that more common word. Now say I, if so be that this be both hurtfull unto them, and yet unavoidable, would not, thinkest thou, the whole it selfe be in a sweet case, all the parts of it being subject to alteration, yea and by their making it selfe fitted for corruption, as consisting of things different and contrarie? And did nature then either of her selfe thus project and purpose the affliction and miserie of her parts, and therefore of purpose so made them, not only that haply they might, but of necessity that they should fall into evill; or did not shee know what shee did, when shee made them? For either of these two to say, is equally absurd. But to let passe nature in generall, and to reason of things particular according to their owne particular natures; how absurd and ridiculous is it, first to say that all parts of the whole are, by their proper naturall constitution, subject to alteration; and then when any such thing doth happen, as when one doth fall sick and dyeth, to **Change** take on and wonder as though some strange thing **in human** had happened? Though this besides might **bodies** moove not so grievously to take on when any such thing doth happen, that whatsoever is dissolved, it is dissolved into those things, whereof it was compounded. For every dissolution is either a meere dispersion, of the Elements into those Elements againe whereof every thing did consist, or a change, of that which is more solid into Earth; and of that which is pure and subtill or spirituall, into aire. So that by this meanes nothing is lost, but all resumed againe into those rationall generative seeds of the Universe; and this Universe, either after a certaine period of time to be consumed by fire, or by continuall changes to bee renued, and so for ever to endure. Now that solid and Spirituall that wee speak of, thou must not conceive it to be that very same, which at first was, when thou wert borne. For alas! all this that now thou art in either kinde, either for matter of substance, or of life, hath but two or three dayes agoe partly from meates eaten, and partly from aire breathed in, received all its influxe, being the same then in no other respect, then a running river, maintained by the perpetuall influxe and new supply of waters, is the same. That therefore which thou hast since received, not that which came from thy Mother, is that which comes to change and corruption. But suppose that that for the generall substance, and more solid part of it, should still cleave unto thee

Take heed never so close, yet what is that to the proper qualities, and affections of it, by which persons are distinguished, which certainly are quite different?

VIII. Now that thou hast taken these names upon thee of good, modest, true; of ἔμφρων, σύμφρων, ὑπέρφρων; take heed least at any times by doing any thing that is contrarie, thou be but improperly so called, and lose thy right to these appellations. Or if thou doe, return unto them again with all possible speed. And remember, that the word ἔμφρων notes unto thee an intent and intelligent consideration of every object that presents it selfe unto thee, without distraction. And the word σύμφρων, a ready and contented acceptation of whatsoever by the appointment of the common nature, happens unto thee. And the word ὑπέρφρων, a super-extention, or a transcendent, and outreaching disposition of thy minde, whereby it passeth by all bodily paines and pleasures, honour and credit, death and whatsoever is of the same Nature, as matters of absolute indifferencie, and in no wise to be stood upon by a wise man. These then if inviolably thou shalt observe, and shalt not be ambitious to be so called by others, both thou thy selfe shalt become a new man, and thou shalt begin a new life. For to continue such as hitherto thou hast beene, to undergoe those distractions and distempers as thou must needes for such a life as hitherto thou hast lived, is the part of one that is very foolish, and is overfond of his life. Whom a man might compare to one of those halfe-eaten wretches, matched in the Amphitheatre with **The Isles** wild beasts; who as full as they are all the body **of the** over with wounds and blood, desire for a great **Blest** favour, that they may be reserved till the next day, then also, and in the same estate to bee exposed to the same nayles and teeth as before. Away therefore, ship thy selfe, and from the troubles and distractions of thy former life convay thy selfe as it were unto these few Names; and if thou canst abide in them, or be constant in the practice and possession of them, continue there as glad and joyfull as one that were translated unto some such place of blisse and happinesse as that which by Hesiod and Plato is called the Ilands of the Blessed, by others called The Elysian Fields. And whensoever thou findest thy selfe, that thou art in danger of a relapse, and that thou art not able to master and overcome those difficulties and temptations that present themselves in thy present station: get thee into any private corner, where thou mayest be better able. Or if that will not serve, forsake even thy life rather. But so that it be not in passion, but in a plaine voluntary modest way: this being the onely commendable action of thy whole life, that thus thou art departed, or this having beene the maine worke and businesse of thy whole life, that thou mightest thus depart. Now for the better remembrance of those names that we have spoken of, thou shalt finde it a very good helpe, to remember the Gods as often as may be; and that, the thing which they require at our hands, of as many of us, as are by nature reasonable creatures; is not that with faire words, and outward shew of piety and devotion we should flatter them, but that we should become like unto them: and that as all other naturall creatures, the Figge tree for example; the Dogge, the Bee; both doe, all of them, and apply themselves unto that, which by their naturall constitution, is proper unto them; so man likewise should doe that, which by his Nature, as he is a man, belongs unto him.

The daily slavery

IX. Toyes and fooleries at home; warres abroad: sometimes terror, sometimes torpor, or stupid sloath: this is thy dayly slaverie. By little and little if thou doest not better looke to it, those sacred Dogmata will be blotted out of thy minde. How many things be there, which when as a meere naturalist, thou hast barely considered of according to their nature, thou doest let passe without any further use? Whereas thou shouldst in all things so joyne action and contemplation, that thou mightest both at the same time attend all present occasions, to performe everything duly, and carefully; and yet so intend the contemplative part too, that no part of that delight and pleasure, which the contemplative knowledge of every thing, according to its true nature doth of it selfe afford, might be lost. Or, that the true and contemplative knowledge of every thing according to its owne nature, might of it selfe, (action being subject to many lets and impediments) afford unto thee sufficient pleasure and happinesse. Not apparent indeede, but not concealed. And when shalt thou attaine to the

happinesse of true simplicity, **and** unaffected
gravity? When shalt thou rejoyce in the certaine knowledge of every particular object according to its true Nature: as what the matter
and substance of it is; what use it is for in the
world: how long it can subsist: what things it
doth consist of: who they be that are capable of
it, and who they that can give it, and take it
away?

Predatory instincts

X. As the Spider, when it **hath** caught the
Fly that it hunted after, is not little proud, nor
meanely conceited of her selfe: as hee likewise
that hath caught an Hare, or hath taken a Fish
with his net: as another for the taking of a
Boare, and another of a Beare: so may they be
proud, and applaud themselves for their valiant
acts against the Sarmatæ, or Northern Nations
lately defeated. For these also, these famous
souldiers and warlike **men**, if thou dost looke
into their mindes and opinions, what doe they
for the most part but hunt after prey?

XI. To finde out, and set to thy selfe some
certain way and method of contemplation,
whereby thou mayest clearely discerne and represent unto thy selfe, the mutuall change of all
things, the one into the other. Beare it in thy
minde evermore, and see that thou be throughly
well exercised in this particular. For there
is not any thing more effectuall to beget true
magnanimity.

XII. He hath got loose from, or, hee hath
shaken off the bonds of his body, and perceiving
that within a very little while hee must of neces-

sity bid the World farewell, and leave all these things behinde him, hee wholy applied himselfe, as to righteousnesse in all his actions, so to the common Nature in all things that should happen unto him. And contenting himselfe with these two things, to doe all things justly, and whatsoever God doth send to like well of it: what others shall either say or thinke of him, or shall doe against him, hee doth not so much as trouble his thoughts with it. To goe on straight, whither right and reason directed him, and by so doing to follow God, was the onely thing that hee did minde, that, his onely businesse and occupation.

What use in mistrust?

XIII. What use is there of suspition at all? or, why should thoughts of mistrust, and suspition concerning that which is future, trouble thy minde at all? What now is to be done, if thou mayest search and enquire into that, what needes thou care for more? And if thou art well able to perceive it alone, let no man divert thee from it. But if alone thou doest not so well perceive it, suspend thine action, and take advice from the best. And if there bee any thing else that doth hinder thee, goe on with prudence and discretion, according to the present occasion and opportunity, still proposing that unto thy selfe, which thou doest conceive most right and just. For to hit that aright, and to speed in the prosecution of it, must needes be happinesse, since it is that onely which wee can truely and properly be said to misse of, or, miscarrie in.

XIV. What is that that is slow, and yet

quick ? merry and yet grave ? Hee that in all things doth follow Reason for his guide.

Give what thou wilt

XV. In the morning as soone as thou art awaked, when thy judgement, before either thy affections, or externall objects have wrought upon it, is yet most free and impartiall : put this question to thy selfe, whether if that which is right and just be done, the doing of it by thy selfe, or by others when thou art not able thy selfe, be a thing materiall or no. For sure it is not. And as for these that keepe such a life, and stand so much upon the praises, or dispraises of other men, hast thou forgotten : what manner of men they be ? that such and such upon their beds, and such at their board : what their ordinary actions are : what they pursue after, and what they fly from : what thefts and rapines they commit, if not with their hands and feet, yet with that more precious part of theirs, their mindes : which (would it but admit of them) might enjoy faith, modesty, truth, justice, a good spirit.

XVI. Give what thou wilt, and take away what thou wilt, saith he that is well taught and truly modest, to Him that gives, and takes away. And it is not out of a stout, and peremptory resolution, that he saith it, but in meere love, and humble submission.

XVII. So live as indifferent to the world, and all worldly objects, as one who liveth by himselfe alone upon some desert hill. For whether here, or there, if the whole world be but as one Towne, it matters not much for the place. Let

<small>Being better than seeming</small> them behold, and see a Man, that is a Man indeede, living according to the true nature of man. If they cannot beare with me, let them kill me. For better were it to die, then so to live as they would have thee.

XVIII. Make it not any longer a matter of dispute, or discourse, what are the signes and proprieties of a good man, but really, and actually to be such.

XIX. Ever to represent unto thy selfe, and to set before thee, both the generall Age, and Time of the World, and the whole Substance of it. And how all things particular in respect of these are for their substance, as one of the least seedes that is, or, as the seede that is in a Figge: and for their duration, as the turning of the pestle in the Morter once about. Then to fix thy minde upon every particular object of the World, and to conceive it, (as it is indeed,) as already being in the state of dissolution, and of change; tending to some kinde of either putrifaction or dispersion; or whatsoever else it is, that is the death as it were of every thing in his owne kinde.

XX. Consider them through all actions and occupations, of their lives: as when they eate, and when they sleepe: when they are in the act of necessary exoneration, and when in the act of lust. Againe, when they either are in their greatest exultation; and in the middle of all their pompe and glory; or being angry and displeased, in great state and majestie, as from an higher place, they chide and rebuke. How

base, and slavish, but a little while agoe, they **Natural**
were faine to be, that they might come to this; **love**
and within a very little while what will bee their
estate, when death hath once seazed upon them.

XXI. That is best for every one, that the
common Nature of all doth send unto every one,
and then is it best, when she doth send it.

XXII. The Earth, saith the Poet, doth often
long after the raine. So is the glorious skie often
as desirous to fall upon the earth, which argues a
mutuall kinde of love betweene them. And so
(say I) doth the world beare a certaine affection
of love to whatsoever shall come to passe. With
thine affections shall mine concurre, O World.
The same (and no other,) shall the object of
my longing be, which is of thine. Now that the
World doth love, as it is true indeede, so is it as
commonly said, and acknowledged, when, according
to the Greeke phrase, imitated by the
Latines, of things that use to be, wee say commonly,
that they love to be.

XXIII. Either thou doest continue in this
kinde of life, and that is it, which so long thou
hast beene used unto and therefore tolerable: or
thou doest retire, or leave the World, and that
of thine owne accord, and then thou hast thy
minde: or thy life is cut off, and then mayest
thou rejoyce that thou hast ended thy charge.
One of these must needes be. Be therefore of
good comfort.

XXIV. Let it alwayes appeare, and be manifest
unto thee, that solitarinesse, and desart
places, by many Philosophers, so much esteemed

Law the Dispenser of, and affected, are of themselves but thus and thus; and that all things are here to them that live in Townes, and converse with others: as they are the same nature every where to be seene and observed: to them that have retired themselves to the top of mountaines, and to desart Havens, or what other desart and inhabited places soever. For any where if thou wilt mayest thou quickly finde and apply that to thy selfe, which Plato saith of his Philosopher, in a place; as private and retired saith hee, as if hee were shut up and enclosed about in some Shepherds lodge, on the top of a hill. There by thy selfe to put these questions to thy selfe, or to enter into these considerations: What is my chiefe and principall part, which hath power over the rest? What is now the present estate of it, as I use it; and what is it, that I employ it about? Is it now voyde of reason or no? Is it free, and separated; or so affixed, so congealed and growne together, as it were with the flesh, that it is swayed by the motions and inclinations of it?

XXV. He that runnes away from his Master, is a fugitive. But the law is every mans Master. He therefore that forsakes the Law, is a fugitive. So is hee, whosoever he be, that is either sorry, angry, or afraid, or for any thing that either hath beene, is, or shall be by his appointment, who is the Lord and Governour of the Universe. For hee truly and properly is Νόμος, or the Law, as the onely νέμων or, distributer and dispenser of all things that happen unto any one in his life time. Whatsoever then is either sorry, angry, or afraid, is a fugitive.

Small beginnings

XXVI. From man is the seede, that once cast into the wombe, man hath no more to doe with it. Another Cause succeedeth, and undertakes the Worke, and in time brings a Child (that wonderfull effect from such a beginning!) to perfection. Againe, Man lets food downe through his throat; and that once downe, hee hath no more to doe with it. Another Cause succeedeth and distributeth this foode into the Senses, and the affections: into life, and into strength; and doth with it those other many and marvailous things, that belong unto man. These things therefore that are so secretly, and invisibly wrought and brought to passe, thou must use to behold and contemplate; and not the things themselves onely, but the power also by which they are effected; that thou mayst behold it, though not with the eyes of the body, yet as plainly and visibly as thou canst see and discerne the outward efficient cause of the depression and elevation of any thing.

XXVII. Ever to mind and consider with thy selfe, how all things that now are, have beene heretofore much after the same sort, and after the same fashion that now they are: and so to thinke of those things which shall bee hereafter also. Moreover, whole *dramata*, and uniforme scenes, or scenes that comprehend the lives and actions of men of one calling and profession, as many as either in thine owne experience thou hast knowne, or by reading of ancient histories;

Foolish lamentations (as the whole Court of Adrianus, the whole Court of Antoninus Pius, the whole Court of Philippus, that of Alexander, that of Crœsus: to set them all before thine eyes. For thou shalt finde that they are all but after one sort and fashion: only that the actors were others.

XXVIII. As a pigge that cryes and flings when his throat is cut, phancie to thy selfe every one to bee, that grieves for any worldly thing and takes on. Such a one is he also, who upon his bed alone, doth bewaile the miseries of this our mortall life. And remember this, that unto reasonable creatures only it is granted that they may willingly and freely submit unto Providence: but absolutely to submit, is a necessity imposed upon all creatures equally.

XXIX. Whatsoever it is that thou goest about, consider of it by thy selfe, and aske thy selfe, What? because I shall doe this no more when I am dead, should therefore death seeme grievous unto me?

XXX. When thou art offended with any mans transgression, presently reflect upon thy selfe, and consider what thou thy selfe art guiltie of in the same kinde. As that thou also perchance dost think it a happinesse either to be rich, or to live in pleasure, or to be praised and commended, and so of the rest in particular. For this if thou shalt call to mind, thou shalt soone forget thine anger; especially when at the same time this also shall concurre in thy thoughts, that he was constrained by his error and ignorance so to doe: For how can he choose as long as he is of that opinion? Doe thou therefore if thou canst, take away that from him, that forceth him to doe as he doth.

Worldly things are as the smoke

XXXI. When thou seest Satyro, thinke of Socraticus, and Eutyches, or Hymen, and when Euphrates, thinke of Eutychio, and Sylvanus, when Alciphron, of Tropæophorus, when Xenophon, of Crito, or Severus. And when thou doest looke upon thy self, phancie unto thy selfe some one or other of the Cæsars; and so for every one, some one or other that hath beene for estate and profession answerable unto him. Then let this come to thy minde at the same time; And where now are they all? No where or any where? For so shalt thou at all times be able to perceive how all worldly things are but as the smoake, that vanisheth away: or, indeed, meere nothing. Especially when thou shalt call to minde this also, that whatsoever is once changed, shall never be againe as long as the world endureth. And thou then, how long shalt thou endure? And why doth it not suffice thee, if vertuously, and as becommeth thee, thou mayest passe that portion of time, how little soever it be, that is allotted unto thee?

XXXII. What a subject, and what a course of life is it, that thou doest so much desire to be rid of. For all these things, what are they, but fit objects for an understanding, that beholdeth every thing according to its true nature, to exercise it selfe upon? Be patient therefore, untill that (as a strong stomach that turnes all things

Say and do what is best for this time into his owne nature; and as a great fire that turneth in flame and light, whatsoever thou doest cast into it) thou have made these things also familiar, and as it were naturall unto thee.

XXXIII. Let it not be in any mans power, to say truly of thee, that thou art not truly simple, or, sincere and open, or not good. Let him be deceived whosoever he be that shall have any such opinion of thee. For all this doth depend of thee. For who is it that should hinder thee from being either truly simple or good? Doe thou only resolve rather not to live, then not to bee such. For indeed neither doth it stand with reason that he should live that is not such. What then is it that may upon this present occasion according to best reason and discretion, either be said or done? For whatsoever it be, it is in thy power either to doe it, or to say it, and therefore seeke not any pretences, as though thou wert hindered. Thou wilt never cease groaning and complaining, untill such time as that, what pleasure is unto the voluptuous, be unto thee, to doe in every thing that presents it selfe, whatsoever may bee done conformably and agreeably to the proper constitution of man, or, to man as he is a man. For thou must account that pleasure, whatsoever it bee, that thou mayest doe according to thine owne Nature. And to doe this, every place will fit thee. Unto the *Cylindrus*, or roller, it is not granted to move every where according to its owne proper motion, as neither unto the water, nor unto the fire, nor unto any other thing, that either is meerely naturall, or naturall and sensitive; but not rationall. For many things there be that can hinder their operations. But of the minde and understanding this is the proper priviledge, that according to its owne nature, and as it will it selfe, it can passe through every obstacle that it findes, and keepe straight on forwards. Setting therefore before thine eyes this happinesse and felicity of thy minde, whereby it is able to pass through all things, and is capable of all motions, whether as the fire, upwards; or as the stone downewards, or as the *Cylindrus* through that which is sloping: content thy selfe with it, and seeke not after any other thing. For all other kinde of hindrances that are not hindrances of thy minde either they are proper to the body, or meerely proceed from the opinion, Reason not making that resistance that it should, but basely, and cowardly suffering it selfe to be foiled; and of themselves can neither wound, nor doe any hurt at all. Else must hee of necessity, whosoever he be that meets with any of them, become worse then he was before. For so is it in all other subjects, that that is thought hurtfull unto them, whereby they are made worse. But here contrariwise, man (if he make that good use of them that he should) is rather the better and the more praiseworthy for any of those kinde of hinderances, then otherwise. But generally remember that nothing can hurt a naturall Citizen; that is not hurtfull unto the Citie it selfe, nor any thing hurt the City, that

Of hindrances

As the flower of the field, so he perisheth is not hurtfull unto the Law it selfe. But **none** of these casualties, or externall hinderances, doe hurt the Law it selfe; or, are contrarie to that course of justice, and equitie, by which publick societies are maintained: neither therefore doe they hurt either Citie or Citizen.

XXXIV. As he that is bitten by a mad dog, is affraid of every thing almost that he seeth: so unto him, whom the Dogmata have once bitten, or in whom true knowledge hath made an impression, every thing almost that he sees or reades be it never so short or ordinary, doth afford a good memento; to put him out of all griefe and feare, as that of the Poet, 'The windes blow upon the trees, and their leaves fall upon the ground. Then doe the trees beginne to budde againe, and by the spring time they put forth new branches. So is the generation of men; some come into the world, and others goe out of it.' Of these leaves then thy Children are. And they also that applaud thee so gravely, or, that applaud thy speeches, with that their usuall acclamation, ἀξιοπίστως, O wisely spoken! and speake well of thee, as on the other side, they that stick not to curse thee, they that privately and secretly dispraise and deride thee, they also are but leaves. And they also that shall follow, in whose memories the names of men famous after death, is preserved, they are but leaves neither. For even so is it of all these worldly things. Their spring comes, and they are put forth. Then blows the winde, and they goe downe. And then in lieu of them grow others out of the wood

or common matter of all things, like unto them. **Diseased**
But, to endure but for a while, is common unto **minds**
all. Why then shouldest thou so earnestly either
seeke after these things, or fly from them, as
though they should endure for ever? Yet a
little while, and thine eyes will be closed up, and
for him that caries thee to thy grave shall another
mourne within a while after.

XXXV. A good eye must be good to see
whatsoever is to be seene, and not greene things
only. For that is proper to sore eyes. So must
a good eare, and a good smell be ready for whatsoever is either to be heard, or smelt: and a good
stomach as indifferent to all kindes of food, as a
milstone is, to whatsoever she was made for, to
grinde. As ready therefore must a sound understanding be for whatsoever shall happen. But
he that saith, O that my Children might live!
and, O that all men might commend me for
whatsoever I doe! is an eye that seekes after
greene things; or as teeth, after **that which is**
tender.

XXXVI. There is not any man that is so
happy in his death, but that some of those that
are by **him** when he dies, will be ready to rejoyce
at his supposed calamity. Is it one that was
vertuous and wise indeed? Will there not some
one or other be found, who thus will say to himselfe, Well now at last shall I be at rest from
this Pedagogue. He did not indeed otherwise
trouble us much: but I know well enough that in
his heart, hee did much condemne us. Thus
will they speake of the vertuous. But as for us,

Ready to depart alas! how many things be there, for which there bee many that glad would be to be rid of us. This therefore if thou shalt thinke of whensoever thou dyest, thou shalt die the more willingly, when thou shalt thinke with thy selfe, I am now to depart from that world, wherein those that have beene my neerest friends and acquaintances, they whom I have so much suffered for, so often prayed for, and for whom I have taken such care, even they would have me die, hoping that after my death they shall live happier, then they did before. What then should any man desire to continue here any longer? Neverthelesse, whensoever thou dyest, thou must not be lesse kinde and loving unto them for it; but as before, see them, continue to be their friend, to wish them well, and meekly, and gently to carry thy selfe towards them, but yet so that on the other side, it make thee not the more unwilling to die. But as it fareth with them that die an easie quick death, whose soule is soon separated from their bodies, so must thy separation from them be. To these had nature joyned and annexed me: now she parts us; I am ready to depart, as from friends and kinsmen, but yet without either reluctancy, or compulsion. For this also is according to Nature.

XXXVII. Use thy selfe, as often, as thou seest any man doe any thing, presently (if it bee possible) to say unto thy selfe, what is this mans end in this his action? But begin this course **with** thy selfe first of all, and diligently examine thy selfe concerning whatsoever thou doest.

XXXVIII. Remember, that that which sets **Accidents and properties** a man at worke, and hath power over the affections to draw them either one way, or the other way, is not any externall thing properly but that which is hidden within every mans dogmata, and opinions: That, that is Rhetorick; that is life; that (to speake true) is man himselfe. As for thy body, which as a vessel, or, a case, compasseth thee about, and the many and curious instruments that it hath annexed unto it, let them not trouble thy thoughts. For of themselves they are but as a carpenters axe, but that they are borne with us, and naturally sticking unto us. But otherwise, without the inward cause that hath power to moove them, and to restraine them, those parts are of themselves of no more use unto us, then the shuttle is of it selfe to the weaver, or the pen to the writer, or the whip to the coachman.

The Eleventh Booke

THE naturall properties, and priviledges of a reasonable soule are; That she seeth her selfe; that she can order, and compose her selfe: that shee makes her selfe as she will her selfe: that shee reapes her owne fruits whatsoever, whereas plants, trees, unreasonable creatures, what fruit soever (be it either fruit properly, or analogically only) they beare, they beare them unto others, and not to themselves.

The Reasonable Soul

Againe; Whensoever, and wheresoever, sooner or later, her life doth end, she hath her **owne** end neverthelesse. For it is not with her, as with dancers, and players, who if they be interrupted in any part of their action, the whole action must needes be imperfect: but shee in what part of time or action soever, shee be surprised, can make that which she hath in her hand whatsoever it be, compleat and full, so that she may depart with that comfort, 'I have lived; neither want I any thing of that which properly did belong unto mee.' Againe, she compasseth the whole world, and penetrateth into the Vanity, and meere outside (wanting substance and solidity) of it, and stretcheth her selfe unto the infinitnesse of eternity; and the revolution or restauration of all things after a certaine period of time, to the same state and place as before, shee fetcheth about, and doth comprehend in her selfe; and considers withall, and sees clearly this, that neither they that shall follow us, shall see any new thing, that wee have not seene, nor they that went before, any thing more then wee: but that he that is once come to forty (if he have any wit at all) can in a manner (for that they are all of one kind) see all things, both passed, and future. As proper is it, and naturall to the soule of man to love her neighbour, to be true and modest; and to regard nothing so much as her selfe: which is also the property of the Law: whereby by the way it appeares, that sound reason and justice comes all to one, and therefore that justice is the chiefe thing, that reasonable creatures ought to propose unto themselves as their end.

How to despise music

II. A pleasant song or dance; the Pancratiastes exercise, sports that thou art wont to be much taken with, thou shalt easily contemne; if the harmonious voyce thou shalt divide into so many particular sounds whereof it doth consist, and of every one in particular shall aske thy selfe, whether this or that sound is it, that doth so conquer thee. For thou wilt be ashamed of it. And so for shame, if accordingly thou shalt consider it, every particular motion and posture by it selfe: and so for the wrestlers exercise too. Generally then, whatsoever it be, besides vertue, and those things that proceed from vertue that thou art subject to be much affected with, remember presently thus to divide it, and by this kind of division, in each particular to attain unto the contempt of the Whole. This thou must transfer and apply to thy whole life also.

III. That soule which is ever ready, even now presently (if neede be) from the body, whether by way of Extinction, or Dispersion, or Continuation in another place and estate to be separated, how blessed, and happy is it! But this readinesse of it, it must proceed, not from an obstinate and peremptory resolution of the mind, violently and passionately set upon opposition, as Christians are wont; but from a peculiar judgement; with discretion and gravity, so that others may be perswaded also and drawne to the like example, but without any noyse and passionate exclamations.

Tragedy and Comedy

IV. Have I done any thing charitably? then am I benefitted by it. See that this upon all occasions may present it selfe unto thy mind, and never cease to thinke of it. What is thy profession? to be good. And how should this be well brought to passe, but by certaine Theorems and doctrines; Some concerning the Nature of the Universe, and some concerning the proper and particular constitution of man.

V. Tragedies were at first brought in, and instituted, to put men in minde of worldly chances and casualties: That these things in the ordinary course of nature did so happen: That men that were much pleased and delighted by such accidents upon this stage, would not by the same things in a greater stage be grieved and afflicted: For here you see what is the end of all such things; and that even they that cry out so mournfully to Cithairon, must beare them for all their cries and exclamations, as well as others. And in very truth many good things are spoken by these Poets; as that (for example) is an excellent passage: 'But if so be that I and my two children be neglected by the Gods, they have some reason even for that,' &c. And againe, 'It will but little availe thee to storme and rage against the things themselves,' &c. Againe, 'To reape ones life, as a ripe eare of corne'; and whatsoever else is to bee found in them, that is of the same kinde. After the Tragedie, the *Comœdia vetus*, or ancient Comœdie was brought in, which had the liberty to enveigh against personall vices; being therefore through this her freedome and libertie of speech of very good use and effect, to restraine men from pride and arrogancie. To which end it was, that Diogenes tooke also the same liberty. After these, what were either the *Media*, or *Nova Comædia* admitted for, but meerely, (or for the most part at least) for the delight and pleasure of curious and excellent imitation? It will steale away; looke to it, &c. Why, no man denies, but that these also have some good things whereof that may be one: But the whole drift and foundation of that kinde of Dramaticall Poetry, what is it else, but as we have said?

A man cut off may be joined again

VI. How clearely doth it appeare unto thee, that no other course of thy life could fit a true Philosophers practise better, then this very course, that thou art now already in?

VII. A branch cut off from the continuity of that which was next unto it, must needs be cut off from the whole tree: so a man that is divided from another man, is divided from the whole Society. A branch is cut off by another, but hee that hates and is averse, cuts himselfe off from his neighbour, and knowes not that at the same time he divides himselfe from the whole bodie, or, corporation. But herein is the gift and mercy of God, the Author of this society, in that, once cut off wee may grow together and become part of the Whole againe. But if this happen often the misery is **that the** further a man is runne in this division, the harder he is to be

The fugitive soldier reunited and restored againe: and however the branch which, once cut off, afterwards was graffed in, gardners can tell you is not like that which sprouted together at first, and still continued in the unity of the body.

VIII. To grow together like fellow branches in matter of good correspondence and affection; but not in matter of opinions. They that shall oppose thee in thy right courses, as it is not in their power to divert thee from thy good action, so neither let it be to divert thee from thy good affection towards them. But be it thy care to keepe thy selfe constant in both; both in a right judgement and action, and in true meekenesse towards them, that either shall doe their endeavour to hinder thee, or at least will be displeased with thee for what thou hast done. For to faile in either (either in the one to give over for feare, or in the other to forsake thy naturall affection towards him, who by nature is both thy friend and thy kinsman) is equally base, and much savouring of the disposition of a cowardly fugitive souldier.

IX. It is not possible that any nature should bee inferiour unto art, since that all arts imitate nature. If this be so; that the most perfect and generall nature of all natures should in her operation come short of the skill of arts, is most improbable. Now common is it to all arts, to make that which is worse for the betters sake. Much more then doth the common Nature doe the same. Hence is the first ground of Justice. From Justice all other vertues have their existence. For Justice cannot be preserved, if either **Totus** wee settle our mindes and affections upon worldly **teres** things; or be apt to be deceived, or rash, and **atque** inconstant. **rotundus**

X. The things themselves (which either to get or to avoid thou art put to so much trouble) come not unto thee themselves; but thou in a manner goest unto them. Let then thine owne judgement and opinion concerning those things be at rest; and as for the things themselves, they stand still and quiet, without any noyse or stirre at all; and so shall all pursuing and flying cease.

XI. Then is the Soule as Empedocles doth liken it like unto a Sphere, or Globe, when she is all of one forme and figure: When shee neither greedily stretcheth out her selfe unto any thing, nor basely contracts her selfe, or lies flat and dejected; but shineth all with light, whereby shee does see and behold the true nature, both that of the Universe, and her owne in particular.

XII. Will any contemne me? let him looke to that, upon what grounds he does it: my care shall be that I may never be found either doing, or speaking any thing that doth truly deserve contempt. Will any hate me? let him looke to that. I for my part will be kinde and loving unto all, and even unto him that hates me, whomsoever he be, will I be ready to shew his error, not by way of exprobation, or ostentation of my patience, but ingenuously and meekly: such as was that famous Phocion, if so bee that he did not dissemble. For it is inwardly that these

> Do not protest too much

things must be: that the gods who look inwardly, and not upon the outward appearance, may behold a man truly free from all indignation and griefe. For what hurt can it be unto thee whatsoever any man else doth, as long as thou mayest doe that which is proper and sutable to thine owne nature? Wilt not thou (a man wholly appointed to be both what, and as the common good shall require) accept of that which is now seasonable to the nature of the Universe?

XIII. They contemne one another, and yet they seeke to please one another: and whilest they seeke to surpasse one another in worldly pompe and greatnesse, they most debase and prostitute themselves in their better part one to another.

XIV. How rotten and unsincere is he, that saith, I am resolved to carry my selfe hereafter towards you with all ingenuity, and simplicity. O man, what doest thou meane! what needs this profession of thine? the thing it selfe will shew it. It ought to be written upon thy forehead. No sooner thy voyce is heard, then thy countenance must be able to shew what is in thy mind: even as he that is loved knowes presently by the lookes of his sweet-heart what is in her minde. Such must he be for all the world, that is truly simple and good, as he whose arme holes are offensive, that whosoever stands by, as soone as ever he comes neere him, may as it were smell him whether he will or no. But the affectation of simplicity, is nowise laud-

able. There is nothing more shamefull then per- **Power**
fidious friendship. Above all things, that must **over our**
be avoided. However true goodnesse simplicity **thoughts**
and kindnesse cannot so be hidden, but that as
we have already said in the very eyes and countenance they will shew themselves.

XV. To live happily is an inward power
of the soule, when shee is affected with
indifferencie, towards those things that are
by their nature indifferent. To be thus
affected she must consider all worldly objects
both divided and whole: remembring withall
that no object can of it selfe beget any opinion
in us, neither can come to us, but stands without
still and quiet; but that we our selves beget, and
as it were print in our selves opinions concerning
them. Now it is in our power, not to print
them; and if they creepe in and lurk in some
corner, it is in our power to wipe them off.
Remembering moreover, that this care and
circumspection of thine, is to continue but for
a while, and then thy life will be at an end.
And what should hinder, but that thou mayest
doe well with all these things? For if they be
according to nature, rejoyce in them, and let
them be pleasing and acceptable unto thee.
But if they be against Nature, seek thou that
which is according to thine owne Nature, and
whether it be for thy credit or no, use all possible speed for the attainment of it: for no man
ought to be blamed, for seeking his owne good
and happinesse.

XVI. Of every thing thou must consider

Atoms or Nature? from whence it came, of what things it doth consist, and into what it will be changed: what will be the nature of it, or what it will be like unto when it is changed; and that it can suffer no hurt by this change. And as for other mens, either foolishnesse, or wickednesse, that it may not trouble and grieve thee; First generally thus; What reference have I unto these? and that we are all borne for one anothers good: Then more particularly after another consideration; as a Ram is first in a flock of Sheepe, and a Bull in a Heard of cattell, so am I borne to rule over them. Begin yet higher, even from this: if Atomes be not the beginning of all things, then which to beleeve nothing can be more absurd, then must we needes grant that there is a Nature, that doth governe the Universe. If such a Nature, then are all worse things made for the betters sake; and all better for one anothers sake. Secondly, what manner of men they be, at board, and upon their beds, and so forth. But above all things, how they are forced by their opinions that they hold, to doe what they doe; and even those things that they doe, with what pride and selfe-conceit they doe them. Thirdly, that if they doe these things rightly, thou hast no reason to be grieved. But if not rightly, it must needes be that they doe them against their wills, and through meere ignorance. For as, according to Platoes opinion, no soule doth willingly erre, so by consequent neither doth it anything otherwise then it ought, but against her will. Therefore are they grieved, whensoever they heare themselves charged, either of unjustice, or unconscionablenesse, or covetousnesse, or in generall, of any injurious kinde of dealing towards their neighbours. Fourthly, that thou thy selfe doest transgresse in many things, and art even such another as they are. And though perchance thou doest forbeare the very act of some sinnes, yet hast thou in thy selfe an habituall disposition to them, but that either through feare, or vaine glory, or some such other ambitious foolish respect, thou art restrained. Fiftly, that whether they have sinned or no, thou doest not understand perfectly. For many things are done by way of discreet policy; and generally a man must know many things first, before he be able truly and judiciously to judge of another mans action. Sixtly, that whensoever thou doest take on grievously, or makest great woe, little doest thou remember then that a mans life, is but for a moment of time, and that within a while we shall all bee in our graves. Seventhly, That it is not the sinnes and transgressions themselves that trouble us properly; for they have their existence in their mindes and understandings onely, that commit them; but our owne opinions concerning those sinnes. Remove then, and bee content to part with that conceit of thine, that it is a grievous thing, and **thou** hast removed thine anger. But how should I remove it? How? reasoning with thy selfe that it **is** not shamefull. For if that which is shamefull, be not the onely true evill that is, thou

Reasons against anger

Coals also wilt be driven whilest thou doest **follow**
of fire the common instinct of Nature, to avoyde that
which is evill, to commit many unjust things,
and to become a thiefe, and any thing, that
will make to the attainement of thy intended
worldly ends. Eightly, How many things may
and doe oftentimes follow upon such fits of anger
and griefe; farre more grievous in themselves,
then those very things which we are so grieved
or angry for. Ninthly, That meekenesse is a
thing unconquerable, if it be true and naturall,
and not affected, or hypocriticall. For how
shall even the most fierce and malicious that
thou shalt conceive, be able to hold on against
thee, if thou shalt still continue meeke and loving
unto him; and that even at that time, when hee
is about to doe thee wrong, thou shalt be well
disposed, and in good temper, with all meekenesse to teach him, and to instruct him better?
As for example; My sonne, we were not borne
for this, to hurt and annoy one another; It will
be thy hurt not mine, my sonne: and so to shew
him forcibly and fully, that it is so in very deede:
and that neither Bees doe it one to another, nor
any other creatures that are naturally sociable.
But this thou must doe, not scoffingly, not by
way of exprobation, but tenderly without any
harshnesse of words. Neither must thou doe
it by way of exercise, or ostentation, that they
that are by and heare thee, may admire thee:
but so alwayes that no body be privie to it,
but himselfe alone: yea, though there be more
present at the same time. These nine particular

heads, as so many gifts from the Muses, see that *Quiet*
thou remember well: and begin one day, whilest **strength**
thou art yet alive, to bee a man indeed. But
on the other side thou must take heede, as much
to flatter them, as to be angry with them: for
both are equally uncharitable, and equally hurtfull. And in thy passions, take it presently to
thy consideration, that to be angry, is not the
part of a man, but that to be meeke and gentle,
as it savours of **more** humanity, so of more man-
hood. That in this, there is strength and nerves,
or vigour and fortitude; whereof anger and indignation is altogether voyde. For the neerer
every thing is unto unpassionatenesse, the neerer
it is unto power. And as griefe doth proceed
from weaknesse, so doth anger. For both, both
hee that is angry and that grieveth, have received
a wound, and cowardly have as it were yeelded
themselves unto their affections. If thou wilt
have a Tenth also, receive this Tenth gift from
Hercules the Guide and Leader of **the** Muses:
That is a mad mans part, to looke that there
should be no wicked men in the World, because
it is impossible. Now for a man to brooke well
enough, that there should be wicked men in the
World, but not to endure that any should transgresse against himselfe, is against all equity, and
indeede tyrannicall.

XVII. Foure severall dispositions, or, inclinations there be of the minde and understanding,
which to be aware of, thou must carefully observe: and whensoever thou doest discover them,
thou must rectifie them, saying to thy selfe con-

The Elements themselves obedient to Nature cerning every one of them, This imagination is not necessary; This is uncharitable: This thou shalt speake as another mans slave, or instrument; then which nothing can be more senselesse and absurd: For the Fourth, thou shalt sharply check and upbraid thy selfe, for that thou doest suffer that more divine part in thee, to become subject and obnoxious to that more ignoble part of thy body, and the grosse lusts and concupiscences thereof.

XVIII. What portion soever, either of aire, or fire there be in thee, although by nature it tend upwards, submitting neverthelesse to the ordinance of the Universe, it abides here below in this mixt body. So whatsoever is in thee, either earthy, or humid, although by nature it tend downwards, yet is it against its nature both raised upwards, and standing, or consistent. So obedient are even the Elements themselves to the Universe, abiding patiently wheresoever (though against their Nature) they are placed, untill the sound as it were of their retreate, and separation. Is it not a grievous thing then, that thy reasonable part only should be disobedient, and should not endure to keepe its place: yea though it be nothing enjoyned that is contrary unto it, but that only which is according to its nature? For wee cannot say of it when it is disobedient, as wee say of the fire, or aire, that it tends upwards towards its proper Element, for then goes it the quite contrary way. For the motion of the minde to any injustice, or incontinency, or to sorrow, or to feare, is nothing else but a separation from **nature**. Also when the minde is grieved for any thing that is happened by the divine Providence, then doth it likewise forsake its owne place. For it was ordained unto holinesse and godlinesse, which specially consist in an humble submission to God and his Providence in all things; as well as unto Justice: these also being part of those duties, which as naturally sociable, wee are bound unto; and without which wee cannot happily converse one with another: yea and the very ground, and fountaine indeed of all just actions.

How to be the same man **always**

XIX. He that hath not one and the selfe same generall end alwayes as long as he liveth, cannot possibly be one and the selfe same man alwayes. But this will not suffice except thou adde also what ought to be this generall end. For as the generall conceit and apprehension of all those things which upon no certaine ground are by the greater part of men deemed good, cannot be uniforme and agreeable, but that only which is limited, and restrained by some certaine proprieties and conditions, as of community: that nothing be conceived good, which is not commonly, and publickly good: so must the end also **that** wee propose unto our selves, be common and sociable. For he that doth direct all his owne private motions and purposes to that end, all his actions will be agreeable and uniforme; and by that meanes will be still the same man.

XX. Remember the fable of the countrey mouse and the citie mouse, and the great fright and terror that this was put into.

Good Maxims

XXI. Socrates was wont to call the common conceits and opinions of men, the common Lamiæ, or bugbeares of the world: the proper terrour of silly children.

XXII. The Lacedemonians at their publick spectacula, were wont to appoint seates and formes for their strangers in the shadow, they themselves were content to set any where.

XXIII. What Socrates answered unto Perdiccas, why he did not come unto him, Least of all deathes I should die the worst kinde of death, said he: that is, not able to requite the good that hath beene done unto mee.

XXIV. In the ancient mysticall letters of the Ephesians, commonly called *Ephesiæ litteræ*, there was an Item, that a man should alwayes have in his minde some one or other of the Ancient Worthies.

XXV. The Pythagoræans were wont betimes in the morning the first thing they did, to looke up unto the heavens, to put themselves in minde of them who constantly, and unvariably did performe their taske: as also to put themselves in minde of orderlinesse, or good order, and of purity, and of naked simplicity. For no starre or planet hath any cover before it.

XXVI. How Socrates looked, when hee was faine to gird himselfe with a skinne, Xanthippe his wife having taking away his clothes, and carried them abroad with her, and what he said to his fellowes and friends, who were ashamed; and out of respect to him, did retire themselves when they saw him thus decked.

XXVII. In matter of writing or reading thou

must needs be taught before thou can doe either: **Good**
much more in matter of life. 'For thou art borne **Maxims**
a meere slave, to thy senses and brutish affections';
destitute without teaching of all true knowledge
and sound reason.

XXVIII. 'My heart smiled within me.'
'They will accuse even vertue her selfe, with
hainous, and opprobrious words.'

XXIX. As they that long after figges in
winter when they cannot be had; so are they
that long after children, before they be granted
them.

XXX. 'As often as a Father kisseth his Child,
Hee should say secretly with himselfe' (said
Epictetus,) 'To-morrow perchance shall he die.'
But these words be ominous. No words
ominous (said he) that signifie any thing that is
naturall: In very truth and deed not more
ominous then this, 'To cut downe grapes when
they are ripe.' Green grapes, ripe grapes, dried
grapes, or raisons: so many changes and mutations of one thing, not into that which was not
absolutely, but rather so many severall changes
and mutations, not into that which hath no
being at all, but into that which is not yet in
being.

XXXI. 'Of the free will there is no thiefe or
robber:' out of Epictetus; Whose is this also:
That wee should finde a certaine art and method
of assenting; and that we should always observe
with great care and heed the inclinations of our
mindes, that they may alwayes be with their due
restraint and reservation, alwayes charitable, and

<small>No petty matter at stake</small> according to the true worth of every present object. And as for earnest longing, that wee should altogether avoide it: and to use aversenesse in those things onely, that wholly depend of our owne wills. It is not about ordinary petty matters, believe it, that all our strife and contention is, but whether, with the vulgar, wee should be mad, or by the helpe of Philosophie wise and sober, said he.

XXXII. Socrates said, 'What will you have? the soules of reasonable, or unreasonable creatures? Of reasonable. But what? Of those whose reason is sound and perfect? or of those whose reason is vitiated and corrupted? Of those whose reason is sound and perfect. Why then labour yee not for such? Because we have them already. What then doe yee so strive and contend betweene you?'

The Twelfth Booke

WHATSOEVER thou doest hereafter adspire unto, thou mayest even now enjoy and possesse, if thou doest not envie thy selfe thine owne happinesse. And that will bee, if thou shalt forget all that is past, and for the future, referre thy selfe wholy to the divine providence, and shalt bend and apply all thy present thoughts and intentions, to holinesse and righteousnesse. To holinesse, in accepting willingly whatsoever is sent by the divine providence, as being that which the nature of the Holiness and Righteousness Universe hath appointed unto thee, which also hath appointed thee for that, whatsoever it be. To righteousnesse, in speaking the Truth freely, and without ambiguity; and in doing all things justly and discreetly. Now in this good course, let not other mens either wickednesse, or opinion, or voyce hinder thee: no, nor the sense of this thy pamperd masse of flesh: for let that which suffers, looke to it selfe. If therefore whensoever the time of thy departing shall come, thou shalt readily leave all things, and shalt respect thy minde onely, and that divine part of thine, and this shall be thine onely feare, not that some time or other, thou shalt cease to live, but thou shalt never begin to live according to Nature: then shalt thou be a man indeede, worthy of that world, from which thou hadst thy beginning; then shalt thou cease to be a stranger in thy Country, and to wonder at those things that happen dayly, as things strange and unexpected, and anxiously to depend of divers things that are not in thy power.

II. God beholds our mindes and understandings, bare and naked from these materiall vessels, and outsides, and all earthly drosse. For with his simple and pure understanding, hee pierceth into our inmost and purest parts, which from His, as it were by a water pipe and chanell, first flowed and issued. This if thou also shalt use to doe, thou shalt rid thy selfe of that manifold luggage, wherewith thou art round about en-

The trinity in man cumbred. For hee that does regard neither his body, nor his cloathing, nor his dwelling, nor any such externall furniture, must needes gaine unto himselfe great rest and ease. Three things there be in all, which thou doest consist of; thy body, thy life, and thy minde. Of these the two former, are so farre forth thine, as that thou art bound to take care for them. But the third alone is that which is properly thine. If then thou shalt separate from thy selfe, that is from thy minde, whatsoever other men either doe or say, or whatsoever thou thy selfe hast heretofore either done or said; and all troublesom thoughts concerning the future, and whatsoever, (as either belonging to thy body or life:) is without the jurisdiction of thine owne will, and whatsoever in the ordinary course of humane chances and accidents doth happen unto thee; so that thy minde (keeping her selfe loose and free from all outward coincidentall intanglements; alwayes in a readinesse to depart:) shall live by her selfe, and to her selfe, doing that which is just, accepting whatsoever doth happen, and speaking the truth alwayes; If I say thou shalt separate from thy minde, whatsoever by sympathie might adhere unto it, and all time both past and future, and shalt make thy selfe in all points and respects, like unto Empedocles his allegorical Sphere, 'all round and circular,' &c. and shalt thinke of no longer life, then that which is now present: Then shalt thou bee truly able to passe the remainder of thy dayes without troubles and distractions; nobly and generously disposed, and in good favour and correspondency, with that Spirit which is within thee.

Do the dead live again?

III. I have often wonderd, how it should come to passe, that every man loving himselfe best, should more regard other mens opinions concerning himselfe, then his owne. For if any God or grave Master standing by, should command any of us to think nothing by himselfe, but what he should presently speake out; no man were able to endure it, though but for one day. Thus doe wee feare more what our neighbours will think of us, then what wee our selves.

IV. How comes it to passe, that the Gods having ordered all other things so well and so lovingly, should be overseene in this one onely thing, that whereas there hath beene some very good men, that have made many covenants as it were with God, and by many holy actions, and outward services contracted a kinde of familiarity with Him; that these men when once they are dead, should never be restored to life, but be extinct for ever. But this thou mayest be sure of, that this (if it be so indeed) would never have beene so ordered by the Gods, had it beene fit otherwise. For certainly it was possible, had it beene more just so; and had it beene according to Nature, the Nature of the Universe would easily have borne it. But now because it is not so, (if so be that it be not so indeed) be therefore confident that it was not fit it should be so. For thou seest thy selfe, that now seeking after this matter, how freely thou doest argue and contest with God. But were not the Gods both just and good in the highest degree, thou durst not thus reason with them. Now if just and good, it could not be that in the creation of the world, they should either unjustly, or unreasonably oversee any thing.

What things to meditate upon

V. Use thy selfe even unto those things that thou doest at first despaire of. For the left hand wee see, which for the most part lyeth idle because not used; yet doth it hold the bridle with more strength then the right, because it hath beene used unto it.

VI. Let these be the objects of thy ordinarie meditation: to consider, what manner of men both for soule and body wee ought to be, whensoever death shall surprise us: The shortnesse of this our mortall life: The immense vastnesse of the time that hath beene before, and will be after us: the frailty of every worldly materiall object: all these things to consider, and behold cleerly in themselves, all disguisement of externall outside being removed and taken away. Againe, to consider the efficient causes of all things: the proper ends and references of all actions: what paine is in it selfe, what pleasure, what death: what fame or honour, how every man is the true and proper ground of his owne rest and tranquillity, and that no man can truly be hindered by any other: That all is but conceit and opinion. As for the use of thy Dogmata, thou must carry thy selfe in the practice of them, rather like unto a Pancratiastes, or, one that at the same time both fights and wrastles with

hands and feet, then a Gladiator. For this, Be not
if he lose his sword that he fights with, he is surprised
gone: whereas the other hath still his hand free, at what
which he may easily turne, and manage at his will. is natural

VII. All worldly things thou must behold and consider, dividing them into matter, forme, and reference, or their proper end.

VIII. How happy is man in this his power that hath beene granted unto him: that he needs not doe any thing but what God shall approve, and that he may imbrace contentedly, whatsoever God doth send unto him?

IX. Whatsoever doth happen in the ordinary course and consequence of naturall events, neither the gods, (for it is not possible, that they either wittingly, or unwittingly should do anything amisse) nor men, (for it is through ignorance, and therefore against their wills that they doe any thing amisse) must be accused. None then must bee accused.

X. How ridiculous and strange is hee, that wonders at any thing that happens in this life in the ordinary course of nature!

XI. Either Fate, (and that either an absolute necessity, and unavoidable decree; or a placable and flexible Providence) or All is a mere casuall Confusion, voide of all order and government. If an absolute and unavoidable Necessity, why doest thou resist? If a placable and exorable Providence, make thy self worthy of the divine helpe and assistance. If all be a mere confusion without any Moderator, or Governour, then hast thou reason to congratulate thy selfe, that in such

The vicious man must needs sin

a generall flood of Confusion, thou thy selfe hast obtained a reasonable Facultie, whereby thou mayest governe thine owne life and actions. But if thou beest caried away with the flood, it must be thy body perchance, or thy life, or some other thing that belongs unto them that is caried away: thy minde and understanding cannot. Or should it be so, that the light of a candle indeed is still bright, and lightsome untill it be put out: and should Truth, and Righteousnesse, and Temperance cease to shine in thee whilest thou thy selfe hast any being?

XII. At the conceit and apprehension that such and such a one hath sinned, thus reason with thy selfe, What do I know whether this be a sinne indeed, as it seemes to be? But if it be, what doe I know but that he himselfe hath already condemned himselfe for it? And that is all one as if a man should scratch and teare his owne face, an object of compassion rather then of anger. Againe, that he that would not have a vicious man to sinne, is like unto him that would not have moisture in the figge, nor children to weepe, nor a horse to neigh, nor any thing else that in the course of nature is necessary. For what shall he doe that hath such an habit? If thou therefore beest powerfull and eloquent, remedy it if thou canst.

XIII. If it be not fitting; doe it not. If it bee not true, speake it not. Ever maintaine thine owne purpose and resolution free from all compulsion and necessitie.

XIV. Of every thing that presents it selfe **Rules of** unto thee, to consider what the true nature of it **conduct** is, and to unfold it, as it were, by dividing it into that which is formall : that which is materiall : the true use or end of it, and the just time that it is appointed to last.

XV. It is high time for thee, to understand that there is somewhat in thee, better and more divine then either thy passions, or thy sensual appetites and affections. What is now the object of my minde, is it feare, or suspition, or lust, or any such thing? To doe nothing rashly without some certaine end; let that be thy first care. The next, to have no other end then the common good. For, alas! yet a little while, and thou art no more : no more will any, either of those things that now thou seest, or of those men that now are living, be any more. For all things are by nature appointed soone to be changed, turned, and corrupted, that other things might succeed in their roome.

XVI. Remember that all is but opinion, and all opinion depends of the minde. Take thine opinion away, and then as a ship that hath stricken in within the armes and mouth of the harbour, a present calme; all things safe and steady : a Bay, not capable of any stormes and tempests : as the Poet hath it.

XVII. No operation whatsoever it be, ceasing for a while, can be truly said to suffer any evill, because it is at an end. Neither can he that is the Author of that operation; for this very respect, because his operation is at an end, be said

The world ever fresh and new to suffer any evill. Likewise then, neither can the whole body of all our actions (which is our life) if in time it cease, be said to suffer any evill for this very reason, because it is at an end: nor He truly be said to have beene ill affected, that did put a period to this series of actions. Now this time or certaine period, depends of the determination of Nature: sometimes of particular nature, as when a man dyeth old; but of nature in generall, however; the parts whereof thus changing one after another, the whole world still continues fresh and new. Now that is ever best and most seasonable, which is for the good of the Whole. Thus it appeares that death of it selfe, can neither bee hurtfull to any in particular, because it is not a shamfull thing (for neither is it a thing that depends of our owne will, nor of it selfe contrary to the common good) and generally, as it is both expedient and seasonable to the Whole, that in that respect it must needs be good. It is that also, which is brought unto us by the order and appointment of the divine providence; so that hee whose will and minde in these things runnes along with the divine ordinance, and by this concurrence of his will and minde with the Divine providence, is led and driven along, as it were by God himselfe, may truly be termed and esteemed the Θεοφόρητος, or Divinely led and inspired.

XVIII. These three things thou must have alwayes in a readiness: first concerning thine owne actions, whether thou doest nothing either idly, or otherwise, then justice and equity doe require: **and** concerning those things that happen unto thee externally, that either they happen unto thee by chance, or by providence; of which two to accuse either, is equally against reason. Secondly, what like unto our bodies are whilest yet rude and imperfect, untill they be animated: and from their animation, untill their expiration: of what things they are compounded, and into what things they shall be dissolved. Thirdly, how vaine all things will appeare unto thee when, from on high as it were, looking down, thou shalt contemplate all things upon Earth, and the wonderfull mutability, that they are subject unto: considering withall, the infinite both greatnesse and variety of things aëriall and things cælestiall, that are round about it. And that as often as thou shalt behold them, thou shalt still see the same: as the same things, so the same shortnesse of continuance of all those things. And, behold, These be the things that we are so proud, and puffed up for.

Three Maxims

XIX. Cast away from thee opinion, and thou art safe. And what is it that hinders thee from casting of it away? When thou art grieved at any thing, hast thou forgotten that all things happen according to the Nature of the Universe; and that him onely it concernes, who is in fault; and moreover, that what is now done, is that which from ever hath beene done in the world, and will ever be done, and is now done every where: how neerely all men are allied one to another by a kindred not of blood, nor of seed, but of the same minde. Thou hast also forgotten

Man's mind divine that every mans minde, partakes of the Deity, and issueth from thence; and that no man can properly call any thing his owne, no not his sonne, nor his body, nor his life; for that they all proceed from that One who is the giver of all things: That all things are but opinion; that no man lives properly, but that very instant of time which is now present. And therefore that no man whensoever hee dieth can properly be said to lose any more, then an instant of time.

XX. Let thy thoughts ever runne upon them, who once for some one thing or other, were moved with extraordinary indignation; who were once in the highest pitch of either honour, or calamity; or mutuall hatred and enmity; or of any other fortune or condition whatsoever. Then consider whats now become of all those things. All is turned to smoake; all to ashes, and a meere fable; and perchance not so much as a fable. As also whatsoever is of this Nature, as Fabius Catulinus in the field; Lucius Lupus, and Stertinius at Baiæ; Tiberius at Capreæ: and Velius Rufus, and all such examples of vehement prosecution in worldly matters; let these also runne in thy minde at the same time; and how vile every object of such earnest and vehement prosecution is; and how much more agreeable to true Philosophie it is, for a man to carry himselfe in every matter that offers it selfe, justly, and moderately, as one that followeth the Gods with all simplicity. For, for a man to be proud and high conceited, that he is not proud and high conceited, is of all kinde of pride and presumption, the most intolerable. *I know that there be Gods*

XXI. To them that aske thee, Where hast thou seene the Gods, or how knowest thou certainly that there be Gods, that thou art so devout in their worship? I answer first of all, that even to the very eye, they are in some manner visible and apparent. Secondly, neither have I ever seene mine owne soule, and yet I respect and honour it. So then for the Gods, by the dayly experience that I have of their power and providence towards my selfe and others, I know certainly that they are, and therefore worship them.

XXII. Herein doth consist happinesse of life, for a man to know thoroughly the true nature of every thing; What is the matter, and what is the forme of it: with all his heart and soule, ever to doe that which is just, and to speake the truth. What then remaineth but to enjoy thy life in a course and cohærence of good actions, one upon another immediatly succeeding, and never interrupted, though for never so little a while?

XXIII. There is but one light of the sunne, though it be intercepted by walls and mountaines, and other thousand objects. There is but one common substance of the whole World, though it be concluded and restrained into severall different bodies, in number infinite. There is but one common soule, though divided into innumerable particular essences and natures. So is there but one common intellectuall soule, though it seeme to be divided. And as for all

What other parts of those Generalls which we have
dost mentioned, as either sensitive soules or subjects,
thou these of themselves (as naturally irrationall) have
desire? no common mutuall reference one unto another,
though many of them containe a Mind, or
Reasonable Faculty in them, whereby they are
ruled and governed. But of every reasonable
minde, this the particular nature, that it hath
reference to whatsoever is of her owne kinde,
and desireth to be united: neither can this
common affection, or mutuall unity and correspondency, be here intercepted or divided, or
confined to particulars as those other common
things are.

XXIV. What doest thou desire? To live
long. What? To enjoy the operations of a
sensitive soule; or of the appetitive Facultie?
or wouldst thou grow, and then decrease againe?
Wouldst thou long be able to talke, to thinck
and reason with thyselfe? Which of all these
seemes unto thee a worthy object of thy desire?
Now if of all these thou doest finde that they be
but little worth in themselves, proceed on unto
the last, which is, In all things to follow God
and Reason. But for a man to greeve that by
death he shall be deprived of any of these things,
is both against God and Reason.

XXV. What a small portion of vaste and
infinite eternitie it is, that is allowed unto every
one of us, and how soone it vanisheth into the
generall age of the world: of the common substance, and of the common soule also what a
small portion is allotted unto us: and in what a

little clod of the whole Earth (as it were) it is **How** that thou doest crawle. After thou shalt rightly **small a** have considered these things with thy selfe, **thing** **phancie** not any thing else in the world any **is man!** more to be of any weight and moment but this, to do that only which thine owne nature doth require; and to conforme thyselfe to that which the common Nature doth affoord.

XXVI. What is the present estate of my understanding? For herein lyeth all indeede. As for all other things, they are without the compasse of myne owne will: and if without the compasse of my will, then are they as dead things unto me, and as it were mere smoake.

XXVII. To stirre up a man to the contempt of death this among other things, is of good power and efficacy, that even they who esteemed pleasure to be happines, and payne miserie, did neverthelesse many of them contemne death as much as any. And can death be terrible **to** him, **to whome that only seemes good, which** in the ordinary course of nature is seasonable? **to him, to whome, whether his actions be many or few, so they be all** good, **is** all one; **and who** whether **hee** behold the things of the world being alwayes **the same** either for many years, **or** for few yeares **only, is** altogether indifferent? O man! **as a Citizen** thou hast lived, and conversed **in this** great **Citty** the **World.** Whether just for **so many yeares, or no, what is** it unto thee? Thou hast lived (thou mayest bee sure) as long as the Lawes, and Orders of the City required; **which may be** the common comfort

The play of all. Why then should it be grievous unto
is over thee, if (not a Tyran, nor an unjust Judge,
but) the same nature that brought thee in,
doth now send thee out of the world? As if
the Prætor should fairely dismisse him from the
stage, whom he had taken in to act a while.
Oh, but the play is not yet at an end, there
are but three Acts yet acted of it? Thou
hast well said: for in matter of life, three
Acts is the whole Play. Now to set a certaine time to every mans acting, belongs unto
him only, who as first hee was of thy composition, so is now the cause of thy dissolution. As
for thyselfe, thou hast to do with neither. Goe
thy wayes then well pleased and contented: for
so is He that dismisseth thee.

FINIS

This edition of Casaubon's *translation of* "The Meditations of Marcus Aurelius" *has been edited by* Mr W. H. D. Rouse, *late Fellow of Christ's College, Cambridge. The text has been prepared by a comparison of the first and second editions of* 1634 *and* 1635. *The square brackets of the original, the italics, and a few peculiarities of punctuation have not been reproduced; a parenthetical alternative has now and then been omitted; the spelling of a few proper names has been corrected; but the text is otherwise not altered. Marginalia, Notes, and Vocabulary have* been added by the Editor.

I. G.

Midsummer **Day**, 1898.

Notes

This being neither a critical edition of the text nor an emended edition of Casaubon's translation, it has not been thought necessary to add full notes. Casaubon's own notes have been omitted, because for the most part they are discursive, and not necessary to an understanding of what is written. In those which here follow, certain emendations of his are mentioned, which he proposes in his notes, and follows in the translation. In addition, one or two corrections are made where he has mistaken the Greek, and the translation might be misleading. Those which do not come under these two heads will explain themselves.

It should be borne in mind that Casaubon's is often rather a paraphrase than a close translation; and it did not seem worth while to notice every variation or amplification of the original. In the original editions all that Casaubon conceives as understood, but not exprest, is enclosed in square brackets. These brackets are here omitted, as they interfere with the comfort of the reader. We, moreover, are concerned rather with the style and vigour of the translation than with literal correctness.

Numbers in brackets refer to the Teubner text of Stich. References in the Preface have been altered to suit the same edition, but the divisions of the text are left unaltered. For some of the references identified I am indebted to Mr G. H. Rendall's *Marcus Aurelius*.

    xvii. So plausible, etc. Lucian in Hermotimo, and Is. C. ad ista **Pers.** *Si Cynico barbam petulans, &c., page* 165.—C.

    xix. For my part: See Hugo Grot. *de jure* **Belli ac** P. lib. i., cap. 2, sec. **6.**—C.

    xxxiii. ff. The Greek quotations from this place to the end of the preface are given in full by C., but here are generally reduced to first and last words, or those only which are necessary

NOTES

BOOK I

p. 2. "Both to frequent" (4). Gr. τὸ μή, C. conjectures τὸ μὲ. The text is probably right: "I did not frequent public lectures, **and I was** taught at home."

p. 4. Idiots. . . . Philosophers (9). The reading is doubtful, but the meaning seems **to** be: "simple and unlearned men."

p 6. "Claudius Maximus" (15). The reading of the Palatine MS. (now lost) was παράκλησις Μαξίμου, which C. supposes to conceal the letters κλ as an abbreviation of Claudius.

p. 8. "Patient hearing. . . . He would not" (16). C. translates his conjectural reading ἐπίμονον ἄλλου. οὐ προαπέστη. . . . Stich **suggests a** reading with much the same sense: . . . ἐπίμονον. ἀλλ' οὗτοι. . . .

"Strict and rigid dealing" (16). C. translates τονῶν (*Pal.* MS.) as though from τόνος, **in** the sense of "strain," "rigour." The reading of other MSS. τινῶν is preferable.

p. 13. "Caieta" (17). The passage is certainly corrupt. C. spies a reference to Chryses praying by the sea-shore in the *Iliad*, and supposes M. Aurelius to have done the like. None of **the** emendations suggested is satisfactory.

p. **13.** At xv. Book II. is usually reckoned to begin.

BOOK II

p. 17. "Doe, soule" (6). If the received reading be right, it must be sarcastic; but there are several variants which show how unsatisfactory it is. C. translates εὖ γὰρ ὁ βίος ἑκάστῳ sc. παρ' ἑαυτῷ, which I do not understand. The sense required is: "Do not violence to thyself, for thou hast not long to use self-respect. Life is not (v. l. οὐ) <long> for each, and this life for thee is all but done."

NOTES

p. 20. "Honour and credit do proceed" (12). The verb has dropt out of the text, but C. has supplied one of the required meaning.

"Consider," etc. (12). This verb is not in the Greek, which means: "(And reason also shows) how man, etc."

BOOK IV

p. 43. "Agathos" (18): This is probably not a proper name, but the text seems to be unsound. The meaning may be "the good man ought . . ."

p. 54. "For herein lyeth all" (43). C. translates his conjecture ὅλον for ὅλα.

BOOK V

p. 67. κατορθώσεις (15): Acts of "rightness" or "straightness."

p. 71. "Roarer" (28): Gr. "tragedian." Ed. 1 has "whoremonger," ed. 2 corrects to "harlot," but omits to alter the word at its second occurrence.

p. 74. "Thou hast . . . them" (33): A quotation from Homer Odyssey iv. 690.

p. 75. "One of the Poets" (33): Hesiod, *Op. et Dies*, 197.

p. 76. xxix. and xxx. (36). The Greek appears to contain quotations from sources not known, and the translation is a paraphrase. (One or two alterations are here made on the authority of the second edition.)

BOOK VI

p. 80. "Affected and qualified" (14): ἕξις, the power of cohesion shown in things inanimate; φύσις, power of growth seen in plants and the like.

p. 83. "Wonder at them" (18): *i.e.*, mankind.

p. 92. "Chrysippus" (42): C. refers to a passage of Plutarch *De Communibus Notitiis* (c. xiv.), where Chrysippus is represented as saying that a coarse phrase may be vile in itself, yet have due place in a comedy as contributing to a certain effect.

NOTES

p. 94. "Man or men ... " (45). There is no hiatus in the Greek, which means: "Whatever (is beneficial) for a man is so for other men also."
§ xlii. There is no hiatus in the Greek.

BOOK VII

p. 102. § ix. (11). C. translates his conjecture μή for ἤ. The Greek means "straight, or rectified," with a play on the literal and metaphorical meaning of ὀρθός.
p. 103. εὐδαιμονία contains the word δαίμων in composition.
p. 106. "Plato" (35): *Republic*, vi. p. 486 A.
p. 108. § xxii. (31). The text is corrupt, but the words "or if it be but few" should be "that is little enough."
p. 109. "It will," etc. (38): Euripides *Bellerophon*, frag. 287 (Nauck).
"Lives," etc. (40): Euripides *Hypsipyle*, frag. 757 (Nauck).
"As long," etc. (42): Aristophanes, *Acharnæ*, 661.
"Plato" (44): *Apology*, p. 28 B.
p. 110. "For thus" (45): *Apology*, p. 28 E.
"But, O noble sir," etc. (46): Plato *Gorgias*, 512 D.
p. 111. "And as for those parts," etc. (50): A quotation from Euripides, *Chrysippus*, frag. 839 (Nauck).
"With meates," etc. (51): From Eurip. *Supplices*, 1110.
p. 115. § xxxiii. (63): "They both," *i.e.*, life and wrestling.
p. 115. "Says he" (63): Plato, quoted by Epictetus, Arr. i. 28, 2 and 22.
p. 116. "How know we," etc. (66). The Greek means: "How know we whether Telauges were not nobler in character than Sophocles?" The allusion is unknown.
p. 116. "Pagus" (66): The word is not a proper name, but means "frost."
"The hardihood of Socrates was famous; *see* Plato, *Symposium*, p. 220.

BOOK X

p. 152. § xxii. (24): The Greek means, "paltry breath bearing up corpses, so that the tale of Dead Man's Land is clearer."

p. 175. "The Poet" (21): Euripides, frag. 898 (Nauck); compare Aeschylus, *Danaides*, frag. 44.

p. 176. "Plato" (23): Theaetetus, p. 174 D.

p. 182. "The Poet" (34): Homer, *Iliad*, vi. 147.
"Wood": A translation of ὕλη, "matter."

p. 185. "Rhetorick" (38): Rather "the gift of speech"; or perhaps the "decree" of the reasoning faculty.

BOOK XI

p. 188. "Cithaeron" (6): Oedipus utters this cry after discovering that he has fulfilled his awful doom. He was exposed on Cithaeron as an infant to die, and the cry implies that he wishes he had died there. Sophocles, *Oedipus Tyrannus*, 1391.

p. 189. "*Nova Comaedia* . . . ," etc. C. has here strayed from the Greek rather widely. Translate: "and understand to what end the New Comedy was adopted, which by small degrees degenerated into a mere show of skill in mimicry."

p. 191. "Phocion" (13): When about to be put to death he charged his son to bear no malice against the Athenians.

p. 201. "My heart," etc. (31): From Homer, Odyssey ix. 413.
"They will" (32): From Hesiod, *Opera et Dies*, 184.
"Epictetus" (34): Arr. i. 11, 37.

p. 202. "Epictetus" (36). Arr. 3, 22, 105.
"Cut down grapes" (35): Correct "ears of corn."

GLOSSARY

This Glossary includes all proper names (excepting a few which are insignificant or unknown), and all obsolete or obscure words.

ADRIANUS, or Hadrian (76-138 A.D.), 14th Roman Emperor.

Agrippa, M. Vipsanius (B.C. 63-12), a distinguished soldier under Augustus.

Ala, armpit, 72.

Alexander the Great, King of Macedonia, and Conqueror of the East, 356-323 B.C.

Antisthenes of Athens, founder of the sect of Cynic philosophers, and an opponent of Plato, 5th century B.C.

Antoninus Pius, 15th Roman Emperor, 138-161 A.D., "one of the best princes that ever mounted a throne."

Apathia, the Stoic ideal was calmness in all circumstances, an insensibility to pain, and absence of all exaltation at pleasure or good fortune.

Apollonius of Alexandria, called *Dyscolus*, or the "Ill-tempered," a great grammarian.

Aposteme, tumour, excrescence, 22.

Archimedes of Syracuse, B.C. 287-212, the most famous mathematician of antiquity.

Aruspices, those who observed omens.

Athos, a mountain promontory at the N. of the Ægean Sea.

Augustus, first Roman Emperor (ruled 31 B.C.-14 A.D.).

BACCHIUS: there were several persons of this name, and the one meant is perhaps the musician.

Brutus (1) the liberator of the Roman people from their kings, and (2) the murderer of Cæsar. Both names were household words.

CÆSAR, C. Julius, the Dictator **and** Conqueror.

Caieta, **a** town in Latium.

Camillus, a famous dictator in the early days of the Roman Republic.

Carnuntum, a town on the Danube in Upper Pannonia.

Cato, called of Utica, a Stoic who died by his own hand after the battle of Thapsus, B.C. 46. His name was proverbial for virtue and courage.

Cautelous, cautious, 142.

Cecrops, first legendary King of Athens.

Charax, perhaps the priestly historian of that name, whose date is unknown, except that it must be later than Nero.

Chirurgion, surgeon, 34.

Chrysippus, B.C. 280-207, a Stoic philosopher, and the founder of Stoicism as **a** systematic philosophy.

Circus, the Circus Maximus at Rome, where games were held. There were four companies who contracted

GLOSSARY

to provide horses, **drivers**, &c. These were called *Factiones*, and each **had** its distinguishing colour: *russata* (red), *albata* (white), *veneta* (blue), *prasina* (green). There was high rivalry between them, and riots and bloodshed not infrequently.

Cithairon, a mountain range N. of Attica.

Comedy, ancient; a term applied to the Attic comedy of Aristophanes and his time, which criticised persons and politics, like a modern comic journal, such as *Punch*. See *Nova Comœdia*.

Consort, concert or harmony, 111.

Crates, a Cynic philosopher of the 4th century B.C.

Crœsus, King of Lydia, proverbial for wealth; he reigned 560-546 B.C.

Cynics, a school of philosophers, founded by Antisthenes. Their texts were a kind of caricature of Socraticism. Nothing was good but virtue, nothing bad but vice. The Cynics repudiated all civil and social claims, and attempted to return to what they called a state of nature. Many of them were very disgusting in their manners.

DEMETRIUS of Phalerum, an Athenian orator, statesman, philosopher, and poet. Born, B.C. 345.

Democritus of Abdera (B.C. 460-361), celebrated as the "laughing philosopher," whose constant thought was "What fools these mortals be." He invented the Atomic Theory.

Dio of Syracuse, a disciple of Plato, and afterwards tyrant of Syracuse. Murdered 353 B.C.

Diogenes, the Cynic, born about 412 B.C., renowned for his rudeness and hardihood.

Diognetus, a painter.

Dispense with, put up with, 119.

Dogmata, pithy sayings, or philosophical rules of life.

EMPEDOCLES of Agrigentum, fl. 5th century B.C., a philosopher, who first laid down that there were "four elements." He believed in the transmigration of souls, and the indestructibility of **matter**.

Entrall, entrail **or organ,** 79.

Epictetus, a famous Stoic philosopher. He was **of** Phrygia, at first a slave, then freedman, lame, poor, and contented. The work called *Encheiridion* was compiled by **a** pupil from his discourses.

Epicureans, a sect of philosophers founded by Epicurus, who "combined the physics of Democritus," *i.e.*, the atomic theory, "with the ethics of Aristippus." They proposed to live for happiness, but the word did not bear that coarse and vulgar sense originally which it soon took.

Epicurus of Samos, 342-270 B.C. Lived at Athens in his "gardens," an urbane and kindly, if somewhat useless, life. His character was simple and temperate, and had none of the vice or indulgence which was afterwards associated with the name of Epicurean.

Eudoxus of Cnidus, a famous astronomer and physician of the 4th century B.C.

GLOSSARY

FORTUIT, chance (adj.), 78.
Fronto, M. Cornelius, a rhetorician and pleader, made consul in 143 A.D. A number of his letters to M. Aur. and others are extant.

GRANUA, a tributary of the Danube.

HELICE, ancient capital city of Achaia, swallowed up by an earthquake, B.C. 373.
Helvidius Priscus, son-in-law of Thrasea Pætus, a noble man and a lover of liberty. He was banished by Nero, and put to death by Vespasian.
Heraclitus of Ephesus, who lived in the 6th century, B.C. He wrote on philosophy and natural science.
Herculaneum, near Mount Vesuvius, buried by the eruption of A.D. 79.
Hercules, p. 197, should be Apollo. *See* Muses.
Hiatus, gape, 89.
Hipparchus of Bithynia, an astronomer of the second century, B.C. "The true father of astronomy."
Hippocrates, of Cos, about 460-357 B.C. One of the most famous physicians of antiquity.

IDIOT, p. xxix., means merely the non-proficient in anything, the "layman," he who was not technically trained in any art, craft, or calling.

LEONNATUS, a distinguished general under Alexander the Great.
Lucilla, daughter of M. Aurelius, and wife of Verus, whom she survived.

MAECENAS, a trusted adviser of Augustus, and a munificent patron of wits and literary men.
Maximus, Claudius, a Stoic philosopher.
Media Comœdia, something "midway" between the Old and New Comedy; see *Comedy, Ancient*, and *Nova Comœdia*.
Menippus, a Cynic philosopher.
Middle things, p. 94. The Stoics divided all things into virtue, vice, and indifferent things; but as "indifferent" they regarded most of those things which the world regards as good or bad, such as wealth or poverty. Of these, some were "to be desired," some "to be rejected."
Muses, the nine deities who presided over various kinds of poesy, music, etc. Their leader was Apollo, one of whose titles is Musegetes, the Leader of the Muses.

Nova Comœdia, the New Attic Comedy of Menander and his School, which criticised not persons but manners, like a modern comic opera. See *Comedy, Ancient*.

PAGUS, p. 116, a mistranslation; *see* note.
Palæstra, wrestling school, 84.
Pancratiast, competitor in the pancratium, a combined contest which comprised boxing and wrestling.
Parmularii, gladiators armed with a small round shield (*parma*).
Pesle mesle, pell-mell, 111.
Philippus, founder of the Macedonian supremacy, and father of Alexander the Great.

GLOSSARY

Phocion, an Athenian general and statesman, a noble and high-minded man, 4th cent. B.C. He was called by Demosthenes "the pruner of my periods." He was put to death by the State in 317, on a false suspicion, and left a message for his son "to bear no grudge against the Athenians."

Plato of Athens, 427-347 B.C. He used the dialectic method invented by his master Socrates. He was perhaps, as much poet as philosopher. He is generally identified with the Theory of Ideas; that things are what they are by participation with our eternal Idea.

Platonics, followers of Plato.

Pompeii, near Mount Vesuvius, buried in the eruption of 79 A.D.

Pompeius, Cn. Pompeius Magnus, a very successful general at the end of the Roman Republic (B.C. 106–48).

Praecipitator, juggler, 2.

Pythagoras of Samos, a philosopher, scientist, and moralist of the 6th century B.C.

Quadi, a tribe of S. Germany. M. Aurelius carried on war against them, and part of this book was written in the field.

Rictus, gape, jaws, 26.

Rusticus, Q. Junius, or Stoic philosopher, twice made consul by M. Aurelius.

Salaminius, p. 126, Leon of Salamis. Socrates was ordered by the Thirty Tyrants to fetch him before them, and Socrates, at his own peril, refused.

Sarmatae, a tribe dwelling in Poland.

Sceletum, skeleton, 75.

Sceptics, a school of philosophy founded by Pyrrho (4th cent. B.C.). He advocated "suspension of judgment," and taught the relativity of knowledge and impossibility of proof. The school is not unlike the Agnostic school.

Scipio, the name of two great soldiers, P. Corn. Scipio Africanus, conqueror of Hannibal, and P. Corn. Sc. Afr. Minor, who came into the family by adoption, who destroyed Carthage.

Secutoriani (a word coined by C.), the *secutores*, light-armed gladiators who were pitted against others with net and trident.

Sextus of Chaeronea, a Stoic philosopher, nephew of Plutarch.

Silly, simple, common, 33.

Sinoessa, properly Sinuessa in Latium.

Socrates, an Athenian philosopher (B.C. 469-399), founder of the dialectic method. Put to death on a trumped-up charge by his countrymen.

Spectacula, sights.

Stint, limit (without implying niggardliness). 57.

Stoics, a philosophic system founded by Zeno (4th cent. B.C.), and systematised by Chrysippus (3rd cent. B.C.). Their physical theory was a pantheistic materialism, their *summum bonum* "to live according to nature." Their "wise man" needs nothing, he is sufficient to himself; virtue is good, vice bad, external things indifferent.

Theophrastus, a philosopher,

# GLOSSARY

pupil of Aristotle, and his successor as president of the Lyceum. He wrote a large number of works on philosophy and natural history. Died 287 B.C.

Thrasea, P. Thrasea Pætus, a senator and Stoic philosopher, a noble and courageous man. He was condemned to death by Nero.

Tiberius, 2nd Roman Emperor (14-31 A.D.). He spent the latter part of his life at Capreae (Capri), off Naples, in luxury or debauchery, neglecting his imperial duties.

To-torn, torn to pieces, 84.

Trajan, 13th Roman Emperor, 52-117 A.D.

VERUS, Lucius Aurelius, colleague of M. Aurelius in the Empire. He married Lucilla, daughter of M. A., and died 169 A.D.).

Vespasian, 9th Roman Emperor (9-79 A.D.

XENOCRATES of Chalcedon, 396-314 B.C., a philosopher, and president of the Academy.

www.ingramcontent.com/pod-product-compliance
Lightning Source LLC
Chambersburg PA
CBHW031251250426
43672CB00029BA/2098